D1136000

THE MAN WHO SANK TITANIC

The Troubled Life of Quartermaster Robert Hichens

SALLY NILSSON

The History Press

First published 2011

The History Press
The Mill, Brimscombe Port
Stroud, Gloucestershire, GL5 2QG
www.thehistorypress.co.uk

© Sally Nilsson, 2011

The right of Sally Nilsson to be identified as the Author
of this work has been asserted in accordance with the
Copyrights, Designs and Patents Act 1988.

All rights reserved. No part of this book may be reprinted
or reproduced or utilised in any form or by any electronic,
mechanical or other means, now known or hereafter invented,
including photocopying and recording, or in any information
storage or retrieval system, without the permission in writing
from the Publishers.

British Library Cataloguing in Publication Data.
A catalogue record for this book is available from the British Library.

ISBN 978 0 7524 6071 0

Typesetting and origination by The History Press
Printed in Great Britain

CONTENTS

This book is dedicated to all my family and especially to my boys – my wonderful husband Paul and my sons Hugo and Henry.

ACKNOWLEDGEMENTS

I am very grateful to everyone who has helped me in the writing of this book. I would like to thank the following people: George Behe who spent a considerable amount of time sending me information and advising and sharing his huge knowledge of *Titanic*; Don Lynch who sent me newspaper articles and the letter that I have based the story around; Phillip Gowan who wrote the original biography of Robert Hichens and helped me so much on the family history' Professor Kenneth Plummer from Exeter University who advised me on the complicated subjects of memory and life writing; Louise Berridge, writer and former BBC television producer who I met at The Festival of Writing, who gave advice and encouragement right from the start; Pam Lomax from The Newlyn Archive Centre whose book *Newlyn Before the Artists Came* and advice was so helpful for writing Robert's early life story; Richard Woodman, author of *More Days, More Dollars*, for helping me with valuable crew research; Maria Newbery, Curator of Southampton Maritime Museum, for taking time out of her busy schedule to supply me with important photographs, and thanks too to her colleagues from Southampton Library; Michael Pocock of Maritime Quest for letting me use so many of his photographs of crew and Molly Brown; Bill Wormstedt and Rob Ottmers for letting me use the ice chart and for their excellent work on The Titanic Project; Jonathan from The Titanic Research and Modelling Association for his advice and encouragement; David Brown, author of *Last*

Log of The Titanic, for sending me his detailed account of his theories on the collision; David Bryceson for sending me over images from his book *The Titanic Disaster as reported in the British Press*; Dave Gittins who put me right about helm orders and lots of other useful research; John Chittenden who helped to explain the turning circle of a ship and made a chart for me; Tad Fitch for his *Titanic* passenger information; Tom Golembiewski who sent me very interesting articles about Robert from the Chicago press, and for his encouragement; Brian Ticehurst for his help and the useful information he sent me; Dennis Skillicorn, former Southampton BBC radio presenter, who gave me taped interviews of survivors, his harrowing account of his experience of hypothermia and books on the port city; Steph Roundsmith for sending me a copy of the *Daily Mail* from 20 April 1912; Rick Parsons for his image of Newlyn in the nineteenth century.

And, not forgetting, all my family. I have met so many family members who I didn't know I had and will keep in contact with them from now on: Michael Dyer and family; Neil 'Swanny' Swanson; Elizabeth Cutler who emigrated to Australia; and all from Newlyn. Thanks to Peter and Barbara Clarke in Torquay; to my relatives from Southampton (a huge thank you to Gloria Carey for finding the long-lost photos of Robert's children hidden in the back of her garage); my cousin Amanda Reeves; Sue Neale; Ching and her son, Robert Hichens; also John and Gary Holden. A big thank you to my family who have been so patient and supportive while I have been writing as well as being a mum, wife, daughter and taxi driver.

Thank you.

                                                            Sally Nilsson

⟞✦ INTRODUCTION ✦⟝

At 11.40p.m. on Sunday 14 April 1912, First Officer William Murdoch shouted the order 'Hard-a-Starboard!' to Robert Hichens. For those not nautically minded, starboard means right and port means left. Robert Hichens was the quartermaster and helmsman who, having received the 'Hard-a-Starboard' order, spun the wheel as far as it would go in a desperate attempt to steer *Titanic* away from an iceberg that had been spotted by two lookouts high up in the crow's nest. *Titanic* had been travelling at almost her full speed of 22.5 knots and by the time the iceberg was seen by Murdoch it was less than 500yds away. With the helm 'hard over' *Titanic* veered two points to port but it was not enough for the 882ft-long, 46,000-ton luxury liner to avoid the ice in time. *Titanic* caught the iceberg with a glancing blow on her starboard bow, resulting in such catastrophic damage that the ship foundered and, just over two and a half hours later, she sank. Around 705 passengers and crew were destined to survive but 1,523 perished that night on the freezing north Atlantic.

Robert Hichens, my ancestor, was put in command of lifeboat 6 and given direct orders to row to a ship (thought to be a steamer 5 miles away) to offload his passengers and return. Attempts to reach the steamer failed, though, as her lights moved slowly away into the distance and disappeared. While resting in their lifeboat more than half a mile from where the *Titanic* foundered, as dawn started to break the survivors saw rockets in the direction from where the *Titanic* had sunk and turned to row towards the rescue ship that had fired them, *Carpathia*. They had spent more than seven hours at sea and theirs was the final lifeboat to reach the rescue ship. Robert Hichens was the last man to climb the rope ladder behind the passengers he had seen safely aboard.

There were but a handful of men on duty on deck and in the bridge area on *Titanic* that night. Apart from Robert and William Murdoch they included crow's nest lookouts Fleet and Lee, Sixth Officer Moody, Fourth Officer Boxhall and two other quartermasters, Alfred Olliver and George Rowe. The captain, who was always on duty, had been away from the bridge at the time of the collision. Of these men Captain Smith, Moody and Murdoch went down with the ship. The most senior member of *Titanic* crew to survive the disaster was Second Officer Charles Herbert Lightoller, who would be responsible for telling the world what had happened. He took the stand at both the US and British inquiries and answered hundreds of gruelling questions. Lightoller and more than eighty other witnesses gave their accounts and these statements would be used as the 'true' record for the future, becoming the material for journalists, authors, film producers, historians and researchers for 100 years. The above account is the 'traditional' story of what took place that fateful night. The *Titanic* tragedy was a terrible accident caused by a set of unforeseen circumstances. But what if some of the accounts given at the inquiries were not the full truth? What if some of the witnesses stood at the stand and lied? Why would they do such a thing?

The world wanted to know why it was that *Titanic* was steaming at almost her full speed, directly towards a huge ice field with many icebergs surrounding it – a deadly obstruction. Many ships had reported the field of ice and bergs in the hours, days and weeks before; four of the ships which were following the same tracks or were just miles away, stuck in the ice or diverting to safer waters, had sent messages to *Titanic* with these very ice warnings. Why had a highly skilled senior officer failed to spot the iceberg through his binoculars when it was only 500yds away and directly ahead of them? How could this disaster possibly have happened?

The Senate Committee in America and the Board of Trade in Britain wanted the answers for many questions, but did they ever get the full story? In researching Robert Hichens, I studied the testimonies from key witnesses and found that there were a number of anomalies; the evidence given by some of the officers and crew did not make sense and it appears that these men did not tell the truth, even under oath. I hope to later show that these anomalies are an integral part of Robert Hichens' tale and of *Titanic*'s wider story.

As a result of the sinking and subsequent inquiries, more lifeboats were supplied on liners crossing the Atlantic. Searchlights were put on the ships and extra lookouts were stationed at times when ice was near or visibility compromised. The methods for receiving ice messages were also greatly improved. Other safety measures were put in place and the Inquiry was eventually put to rest. However, no one person or organisation was held directly responsible for the sinking and gradually the story began to disappear from the pages of the newspapers. Myths and legends were born and a plethora of books written on the subject were published over the years, exploring some of the diverse reasons for what could have caused the most famous wreck in maritime history. As so many important witnesses did not survive and only one third of the total passengers and crew were saved, here remains a story that will always be shrouded in some degree of mystery.

We do know that Robert Hichens had been put in command of lifeboat 6, which was the second to be lowered on the port side. In his boat were some of the most wealthy and notable first-class passengers to sail on her maiden voyage. One of them was Margaret Tobin Brown, otherwise known as 'the unsinkable Molly Brown'. If you have seen the 1997 film *Titanic* you may remember the scene in the lifeboat where the crewman (Robert) refuses to go back for survivors and says to Molly Brown in a 'cockney' accent: 'and there will be one less in this boat if you don't shut that hole in your face.'[1] Margaret Brown, three other women and a Canadian colonel were to either testify at the hearings or report in the newspapers that Robert Hichens was a coward and a bully and behaved dreadfully in the boat, refusing to man the oars and go back to pick up those in the water. I am certainly not the only person to have a villainous relative whose behaviour would be best kept in a locked closet of family secrets, but I wanted to know more. I wanted to know why my great-grandfather behaved the way he did. Was he the craven bully who appeared to have lost his mind as these people claimed, or simply a crewman who was following orders and doing his best to save the people in his care?

In researching for this book I have read and digested a great deal of material to get to the bottom of these accusations. To find out about the man himself I also visited and interviewed family members who have been able to give me a feel of what he was really like. Bearing in mind that Robert would be 130 years old now, these family members are second generation, two in their mid-eighties. When I spoke with them I found them to be incredibly helpful, specific and co-operative and there was certainly nothing wrong with their memories.[2] These family members were able to share with me the stories that had been passed to them from their parents and although the Hichens family did not stay close, their narratives were consistent. My great-aunt Dorothy (known as 'Ching') and wife of Robert's youngest son Freddie, was able to help paint a picture of what kind of man Robert was from her husband's accounts. Only one other relative, Barbara, actually met him.

They helped build up a picture of Robert as a conscientious and hardworking seaman, whose family were very proud when he was chosen as one of six quartermasters to join the *Titanic*'s maiden voyage. In fact records show that he was the second quartermaster to be signed on in front of many other hopefuls on the morning of Saturday 6 April. He had served with the Royal Naval Reserves and the Merchant Navy for twelve years, gaining his qualifications and earning the respect of the officers he reported to. Yet as a direct result of everything that happened to him that terrible night on *Titanic*, Robert would be spurned by fellow crewmen, ridiculed in the press and kept away from the family he loved for years. Diagnosed with a post-traumatic mental illness which led to anxiety and depression – fuelled by alcohol – he would eventually try to kill a man and himself, and would serve five years in prison for his crime. Why was Robert affected so badly by his experience on *Titanic*? I was to find out that other crewmen on duty that night had indeed suffered to the same extent, their lives often ending in tragic circumstances too.

I have had the help of some of the most expert and knowledgeable researchers on *Titanic* history in the world, who have helped answer the many questions I have come up against while researching Robert Hichens. It is important to note here that many of these experts hold their own opinions and explanations with regards to the tragedy, which is why the story continues to provoke such important debate and discussions. One of these experts is Don Lynch, a leading historian in *Titanic* history and major contributor for the Titanic Historical Society who worked with James Cameron as historic advisor on the film *Titanic* and has dived to the wreck site to help in his research for his book *Ghosts of the Abyss*. Don is also author of the acclaimed book *Titanic, An Illustrated History*. In this book Don raised an interesting possibility: that Robert could have been 'spirited away' to South Africa by the White Star Line, who owned *Titanic*, in a bid to keep him silent about what he had witnessed that night at the wheel. I wrote to Don to ask him about what he had written and not only did he reply and go on to help me a great deal, but he sent me the astonishing letter shown overleaf which provided him with this information. The letter was written by a man called Thomas Garvey and was given to Don by Garvey's daughter, after his death in 1982. Too much time has passed for anyone to know whether Thomas Garvey tried to get this information to other people during his lifetime, and it appears that, to date, only three people have seen it. Please study the letter: if the content is to be believed (and the evidence I have found strongly suggests it should be), it paints a very different picture to that of the traditional story and tells of gross negligence, conspiracy and lies.

What I found most extraordinary about the letter was that it implied Robert had heard two separate warnings of ice ahead, one from the crow's nest *and* one from the bow, instead of just the call from the crow's nest as I had read in the Inquiry testimonies. Even more worrying was the claim that Robert had then found the first officer lying unconscious on a lounger at the rear of the pilothouse – which was a separate cabin in front of the wheelhouse. The only way Robert could done this, and have shouted in the first officer's ear to try to wake him up as the letter suggests, would have been for him to leave his position at the helm in the wheelhouse and walk/run into the pilothouse to discover the officer. At this pivotal moment there had been no one else in the bridge area. Testimonies show that the two officers who should have been there were absent at this crucial time and the standby quartermaster was performing a duty amidship. Later witness statements reported that after the disaster the crew *were* rounded up and kept under virtual house arrest, and further evidence exists relating to key witnesses being paid for their silence, which you will discover later in the book.

But who was the author of the letter, Thomas Garvey, and the Henry Blum he described? To trace these men, I would first need to find a vessel number for the ship they were on which could then help me find a crew list, but the vessel mentioned in the letter, *Revolution*, had no official number. I started from scratch by trying to find the basics, so I began by researching the Curtis Turbine Experimental and Demonstration ship SS *Revolution* (steam yachts were often prefixed with SS in 1902). In England in 1884 the Hon. Charles Parsons had invented and then developed the first compound steam turbine and by 1894 the first marine turbine was installed in the yacht *Turbina*. The invention was revolutionary and its application was to become universal. Around the same time in America, Charles G. Curtis had also developed a steam turbine using his and the designs of his co-inventor, Carl Gustav de Laval from Sweden. The steam yacht *Revolution* would be the very first vessel in the US to have installed the 'Curtis marine turbine', and Curtis would receive many accolades for his services to the marine industry. An article in the *New York Times* published 4 July 1902 followed the story, which described her trials off Sandy Hook, New Jersey, as highly successful and which created much excitement. The inventor Charles Curtis was on board, as were two prominent marine engineering experts from the Stevens Institute. The *Revolution* was a 178ft yacht that would be used for demonstration purposes in order to promote the steam turbine for the commercial market. It was a luxury vessel with six staterooms, three bathrooms, two deck houses and quarters for nineteen crewmen.

In his letter Thomas Garvey wrote that he and the quartermaster (and helmsman) Henry Blum were crew on the *Revolution* between 1902 and 1903. Although Garvey does not give his rank, his letter suggests that he was of a higher rank than quartermaster. In all probability, only the finest and most experienced men would have been chosen to be crew for such an important and valuable commodity. Henry Blum had also had a long career with the White Star Line, so it should be fair to say that both men would be trusted and professional, with solid reputations – men who weren't given to 'flights of fancy'.

After reading the letter many times, I decided to follow up its claims about the multiple ice warnings and of Robert being silenced and my research started to go in a very different direction.

To Whom It May Concern:

Regarding the S.S. Titanic

In the year 1902-3, we had on board the Curtis Turbine Experimental and Demonstration Ship, S.S. Revolution, an unusually proficient quartermaster, a Norwegian by the name of Henry Blum. He had served on the S.S. Cedric, S.S. Celtic and other White Star Ships.

Henry Blum left the Revolution in 1903 and I didn't see him again until one day in 1924 while browsing on South Street, New York City. He then told me the following:-

While serving as quartermaster on a British ship, they called at Capetown in 1914. The Harbormaster came aboard and after pledging Henry to secrecy for 10 years, related the following account saying he wanted to tell someone to relieve his conscience. He had been, he said, the quartermaster on the Titanic doing his 2 hour trick at the wheel the night of the disaster. He heard the Look-out in the crows nest call out, "Iceberg dead ahead". Seconds later the Bow Look-out called out "Iceberg dead ahead". The First Officer was lying on the lounge at the rear of the pilot house. The Quartermaster said he then shouted the warning in the First Officer's ear but could not awaken him.

He then returned to the wheel and held her steady on her course as he should.

When the survivors were rounded up he was placed under house arrest and spirited away to Capetown. He was given a life long job with good pay for as long as he remained silent.

The promise of secrecy was kept until 1924 when Henry related this and he also said I was the only one he had told this true story to. Norwegians are like that.

I have always believed that the foregoing was true because Henry Blum was a very solid individual and not given to flights of fancy.

Thomas Garvey

Thomas Garvey letter. (Don Lynch)

I found out that other historians already believed and advocated some of what I was just starting to uncover. Another prominent historian, George Behe, had written an incredible piece of detective work in his book *Safety, Speed and Sacrifice*. Behe found evidence of witnesses who spoke of earlier iceberg warnings on the *Titanic*, not just the one solitary berg that had been seen by the lookouts. He also found evidence of key witnesses having been paid for their silence from other resources he had painstakingly researched. I followed the leads George had uncovered and found more in other factual works by well-respected historians, plus many newspaper reports and witness statements, many of which never made it to the inquiries.

By far the most fascinating and thought-provoking research came from testimonies of witnesses at both the *Titanic* inquiries, which I found via the 'US Titanic Project'. From the evidence given in America and Britain and the reports relayed by the lawyers and experts who adjudicated on them, it is possible to get an incredible insight into what passengers and crew witnessed, from the time they joined the ship at her different ports to when they were rescued by the *Carpathia*. You can see for yourself how the crewmen on that fateful night spun their different tales of where they were, what they did and what they saw. Be warned though, the inquiries were huge. Patience and a real interest in the disaster is vital because there are thousands of questions and answers that one can research from more than eighty different witnesses. The books I found to be of the most interest when researching were *Titanic, An Illustrated History* by Don Lynch and Ken Marshall; *Titanic, Triumph and Tragedy* by John Eaton and Charles Haas; *Safety, Speed and Sacrifice* by George Behe; *The Titanic, End of a Dream* by Wynn Crade Wade; *Titanic, R.I.P.* by Diane Bristow and *Titanic Voices* by Donald Hyslop, Alistair Forsyth and Sheila Jemima.

In isolation it would be easy to believe that the above reports were second-hand news, not reliable, hearsay or just plain yahoo. I would have agreed if it were not for the fact that there were so many testimonies and histories that, although unrelated, were saying the same things. When the puzzle started to come together and more pieces began to fit, a different account evolved: a story of conspiracy and cover up; of lies and the lives of innocent men ruined because of the guilt and shame they had to carry with them to hide what had really happened that fateful night. Could it really be possible that a senior officer had neglected his duty on a freezing bridge, while his captain and other officers ignored the warnings of danger directly ahead, and were away from the positions they should have been stationed at in the minutes before a devastating collision? The Thomas Garvey letter shows evidence of a different set of events to those generally believed from the 'traditional' story. I made the decision to use this evidence in my retelling of the events that happened on Sunday 14 April 1912, and in doing so hope to show with my own research the huge part Robert Hichens played in this historic drama, and how what he witnessed on *Titanic* affected the rest of his life. It is of course for you the reader to decide which story you believe.

For Robert's early life I visited Newlyn, Cornwall, and immersed myself in the history and the way of life of the major fishing harbour he grew up in. I spoke to historians at the Morrab Library and at the Newlyn Archive Centre to understand what it would have been like to live there in the late nineteenth century. Again, new family members who I met and have corresponded with were able to tell me about the lives of the people of Newlyn and of the Hichens' household: where they lived and what they were like. I spoke to the older locals in the pubs, to fishermen (one night in the bowels of an old trawler), and attended church where I was able to glean invaluable research about the community, which in some ways has not changed at all over the years. Local history books gave me the extra detail I needed.

Many hours were spent at the Southampton Library and archives where extensive material was made available for me to research the port city, its history and the lives of the people who lived there. Research on *Titanic* also came from websites such as Encyclopedia Titanica, the Titanic Historical Society and Titanic-Titanic.com, and in the other books I have used, all of which are listed in the bibliography. Of course the Internet has uncovered a wealth of information and without it I could not have even started writing. The later, harrowing account of Robert's attempted murder charge comes from the detailed reports of his trial, which was captured in all its grim detail in the newspapers that chronicled the events in Torquay in 1933.

In researching Robert's last legacy at sea, I learned of the role our merchant seamen played during the Second World War. I never fully comprehended before how they steamed across the Atlantic delivering and bringing back goods vital for our country while in constant fear of attack by enemy aircraft and the wolves of the sea, the U-boats. Researching the part Robert played on his final voyage on a cargo ship was a compelling and poignant reminder of a period of history that should never be forgotten,

Titanic was just *one* part of Robert's life – a life which you will see was full of adventure, determination, failure and success. In writing this book I aim to put the record straight and give the most comprehensive account of a man who for a century has been greatly misunderstood. His story begins in a small fishing town in the south-west corner of England in 1882.

1

⟹+ NEWLYN +⟸

The year 1882 was a significant one for the people of Newlyn. Work had started on the new 40-acre harbour in the north-west corner of Mount's Bay, overlooked from the east by the towering battlements of St Michael's Mount, a rocky outcrop a mile out to sea. Newlyn port boasted one of the largest fishing fleets in the United Kingdom, its position offering protection from prevailing westerly winds and the huge gales they could bring. The new harbour would attract further boats from far and wide that would be able to land their catch at almost any time of the year in her safe waters.

For the fishermen of Newlyn it would be pilchards and mackerel that would bring in their main source of income. Packed into casks called hogsheads, the pilchards left from the new Penzance railway station for London and from there went across the country or were exported to their largest customer, Italy. But these stocks were becoming depleted and the small luggers, known as the swallows of the sea, were starting to be replaced by larger mackerel drivers with bigger crews which were capable of much longer fishing expeditions, and whose men would be away for months at a time in their search for the larger quarry. Many families operated a share system as the mackerel drivers were expensive to maintain. It was with a crew of nine that Phillip Hichens sailed from Newlyn, along the west coast of Britain, up to Scotland and down to the north-east town of Whitby. It was on one of his trips to this Yorkshire fishing port that Phillip met

Rebecca Ward. Whitby had many similarities to Newlyn so their union was a natural one, and before long Rebecca, aged twenty, gave birth to their first son Phillip. In 1881, a year later, Rebecca left Whitby with Phillip and their son to start a new life in the small Cornish town.

In this deeply religious community of Celts with its clan mentality Rebecca's initiation would be tough. Her son, who had been born out of wedlock, would be raised by another family and not return to his parents until he was a teenager. The families of Newlyn and the community were so tight-knit that you needed to ask permission just to join in a chat taking place on the cliff; there would be men standing around in their bowler hats called 'mullers' and some of the more daring types chewing on tobacco. On 16 September 1882 Rebecca welcomes her second son, Robert, and it would be he who took the role as eldest son in the Hichens house. Large families were normal in Newlyn, some with up to twelve children, and the Hichens were no exception. Over the next eighteen years Rebecca and Phillip would raise ten children, three girls and seven boys.

The year 1882 was the year the artists began to arrive. Attracted by cheap accommodation and an abundance of free models, the 'Newlyn School' enjoyed a different environment from the industrial cities many had come from and artists painted *en plein air* – outdoors. The growing colony took their inspiration from the rural livelihoods of the hard-working fishing community. The whitewashed terraced cottages interlaced with steep cobbled lanes, the beautiful fishing boats with their brown square sails returning with their catch to be met by jousters, the horse and carts waiting patiently on the beach – all provided ample subject material for their paintings. With the backdrop of crimson sunsets on a sea as flat as glass, or a tempestuous storm with waves crashing over the harbour walls, the artists produced masterpieces which made their way to the lucrative London scene or, on a smaller scale, were bartered with the locals in exchange for boarding and meals.

Young Robert Hichens and the children he played with would have been blissfully unaware of their parents' constant struggles in their tough environment. For them, Newlyn was the best playground ever: the labyrinth of lanes in which to hide, the cliffs and nearby fields to chase each other and the long promenade of nearby Penzance – all these things would have heightened their imaginations. When the fishing boats returned the children waited with their mothers, siblings and extended family for the boats to land their catch on the beach; it was up to everyone to help carry the heavy baskets of fish up the steep Gwavas slip and, for Robert's family, on to the courtyard of St Peter's Square ready to be unloaded down into the cellar beneath their cottage for processing.

There were many harsh times to be faced when unpredictable weather or scarcity of fish meant lower wages to share among the nine-man crew, and it was down to Robert's mother and others like her to plan for the weeks or months ahead. Soups, stews and hot meals of meat and cabbage would be replaced with less appealing alternatives. The shoreline offered limpets and winkles known as 'trigmeat' and dried, salted fish called 'towrag' hung from rafters in readiness in the cellars; not the most favoured of meals for the children of Newlyn. Stocks of flour enabled Rebecca and the other wives to make dough which would be taken up to the communal bake houses where the women would chat while the children played at their feet in the warm aroma of buns, bread and cake. Rebecca and the other women ran the family home with the help of their daughters. Their tough work included mending nets, oiling sou'westers and washing cookware and bedding the men brought home from their trips, as well as all the clothes and linen from their own homes. Once a week the women would gather again with their sopping washing to join at the large and cumbersome neighbourhood mangle or meet in the fields nearby to hang sheets from the bushes to dry.

By 1890 there were three schools in the Newlyn area and the one Robert and his brothers and sisters attended was the Newlyn Board School. It had been built ten years before and stood on top of Newlyn Hill. The sound of the bell tolling could be heard across the bay and for miles around and getting there meant a steep climb up St Peter's Hill and along Church Lane – luckily there was a drinking fountain in the shape of a gun barrel (which the children would inevitably fight over). From there it was further still, through a field with an old mine shaft, round a bend and eventually they arrived. The boys and girls would separate to their own classrooms and the school day would begin from 9a.m., with a break at lunch, until 4p.m. Children were encouraged to be high achievers and although the curriculum was limited, Robert benefited from a good standard of education in an era when schooling for the masses was in its infancy.

Along with school, play and helping with the family chores, Robert and his siblings took part in another community pastime: going to church. Indeed the Primitive Methodist religion found its roots in Newlyn in the 1820s. The community as a whole was attracted by the sermons, which were preached in words everyone could understand, and by the hymns that included strong repetitive choruses and rich harmonies that the Cornish, with their love for singing, enjoyed every Sunday. Just a short walk from their home in St Peter's Square, the Hichens clan would arrive en masse for Sunday service at the Ebenezer Methodist Chapel in Boase Street, and then return home for their day of rest. Robert's uncle Frederick was so entrenched in the religion that he and others like him became missionaries, and Frederick eventually emigrated with his wife and children to set up a mission in Australia.

As children Robert and his siblings were not allowed out on a Sunday unless it was to go to Sunday school; when they were older they were permitted to meet friends for a couple of hours in the evening on the cliff overlooking the bay. It wasn't a proper cliff but a road called Fore Street which overlooked the harbour and Mount's Bay with railings to lean on. Robert was brought up in a community where religion was as much a part of their lives as the fish in the sea. This was a religion where temperance was accepted by all except the few tough young men known as 'hobble-de-hoys' who, when made idle from lack of work, would be liable to misbehave with too much liquor in their stomachs. The tradition of Sunday observance was very strict in Newlyn, and at many of the ports on the west side of Britain, where fishermen put down their nets for the Sabbath day. However, in May 1896 when Robert was fourteen years old, devout Newlyn erupted in crisis, and he witnessed what was to become one of the most infamous events in the town's history, the Newlyn Riots.

Although the fishermen of Newlyn chose not to land fish on the Sabbath, the rule was not observed by the east-coast men predominantly from Lowestoft in Suffolk, known as 'yorkies'. They would regularly land their fish on Sunday and this would attract higher prices than those sold on a weekday, understandably creating a great deal of tension. The situation came to a head on the morning of 18 May 1896, when 1,000 Newlyn men crowded on to the north pier as a dozen or so east-coast boats sailed into the harbour to land their fish. The army of Newlyn men boarded the yorkies' boats and threw their entire catch of 100,000 mackerel into the sea. Other boats, which were moored outside, were also captured and the 'pirates' brought the crews back to town. With many more 'foreigners' waiting out at sea, more help was called for from Newlyns' neighbours at Porthlevan, Mousehole and St Ives.

At this time the whole of Cornwall had little more than 200 policemen for the entire population. Newlyn had never had a perfect relationship with their much larger neighbour, Penzance, but it was to their constabulary a message was sent for police backup, and it was Penzance in turn that called for more policemen to assist from other parts of the county. The situation simmered throughout the course of the day and evening with a few skirmishes, name-calling and brandishing of sticks and stones – but little more. By Tuesday afternoon conditions reached boiling point when word came to Newlyn that a fleet of Lowestoft boats were preparing to land their catch at Penzance. Is response, a mob of 300 men hurried the mile stretch of coast and were met with a throng of police and a tough-looking crowd of Penzance men who were more than happy to fight the Newlyn lads, whatever the cause.

While all this was going on an armada of sailing vessels were sweeping into Mount's Bay with banners flying – the men from Porthlevan, Mousehole and St Ives. It wasn't long, however, before they were joined by a smaller yet much more heavily armed convoy, that of a torpedo-boat destroyer, a gun-boat tender and a special service vessel from the Royal Navy to quell the riots. By land more military had been called for in the form of 330 Red Coats from the Second Battalion of the Royal Berkshire Regiment. For the inquisitive teenage lads of Newlyn, the events unfolding must have been too good an opportunity to miss and they found many vantage points to catch the action, such as the pier, the hills above, the harbour and even the streets surrounding advancing men.

Before long, a pitched battle was in progress, each side using fists, ice axes, barrel staves and stones; any weapon that could be found in the riot. The two sides fought hard, and the strength of the few police was not enough to control the mob. As the fight was reaching its climax, the army of Red Coats arrived, and their pure numbers were eventually enough to beat back the mob and to install martial law, pushing back the men from Newlyn towards their own territory. Roadblocks were put up and by late evening a charged peace was restored and the Penzance men returned to their town. For Robert and the other teenage boys, the riots of Newlyn would have been, without doubt, the most exciting day of their lives so far.

The Navy gunboats remained stationed offshore for a few days, as did the troops barracked nearby, to ensure the troubles did not erupt again. By now the time for violence was over, to be replaced by discussion and a truce, of sorts. The east-coast boats were run by bosses who owned the vessels of the fishermen there, and it was they who demanded the need for fishing on all days of the week. A half-hearted agreement was passed that fishing in Newlyn waters would be permitted on a Saturday but not on a Sunday, and committees in Lowestoft agreed to fish their local waters and only come to Newlyn in bad weather. Still, the arguments for and against carried on through the years until Sunday observance became just a memory for all but the most conscientious of chapel-going fishermen.

Perhaps seeing the Royal Navy's vessels coming into Mount's Bay that Wednesday in May 1896 had an effect on Robert, maybe it was the incredible progress being made in the merchant trade with steam powering ever larger and faster ships, or even the fact that boys who were turning into men were lured by the colourful advertisements for new lives abroad, away from the hardship of fishing. Either way, Robert had been out to sea for four years but when he turned eighteen he was ready to choose a different career to that of his father, and with the help of a state enlistment programme, he left his family to start a career as a trainee in the Royal Naval Reserves.

2

SOUTHAMPTON

Dearest Florence

I now take this opportunity of writing these few lines according to my promise hoping you are none the worse for your nice little walk last night. I only wish I had met you at 5 or 6 o'clock and I would have seen more of you. I suppose you don't know that I have taken rather a fancy to you.

Robert Hichens

Yacht Ariano

Torquay

By 1900 the Royal Naval Reserves (RNR) were enlisting many young men from fishing communities who would be called upon to support the Royal Navy in times of war. After initial on-shore training Robert embarked on his first major placement on the warship HMS *Alexandra*. The *Alexandra* was remarkable in that she was neither fish nor fowl. Although many ships were crossing the Atlantic by steam, age-old traditions still existed and *Alexandra* was not only powered by vertical compound engines and high-pressure boilers, she also had a full rig of sails. She was complemented with an impressive armament of heavy artillery which gave Robert and the other trainees all the experience they could hope for to drive their careers forward.

HMS *Revenge* would be Robert's next training post. A 400ft, 15,000-ton battleship, she was one of the Royal Sovereign Class, considered the most potent of warships in the world; they were only surpassed by the revolutionary Dreadnoughts that would make them obsolete in just two years' time. He and the other recruits of the RNR quickly gained the respect of their counterparts in the Royal Navy for their professionalism, navigation skills and seamanship. Robert knew that if he continued to work hard, building on the opportunity and responsibility that had been given him, there was no reason why he could not be considered for a position of junior officer in just a few years. So that's what he did, and for the next five years he served on different vessels, expanding his knowledge and eventually reaching the position of quartermaster.

In 1905, while on shore leave from the yacht *Ariano*, Robert began an innocent and blossoming relationship with a pretty farm labourer's daughter from nearby Manaton, twenty-year-old Florence Mortimore. They made an interesting couple – Robert was rather short and Florence was quite a bit taller than her beau. They spent as much time as they could together before Robert returned to his duty. It didn't take long for their courtship to flourish and they married at the parish church in Manaton, Devon, on 23 October 1906. They rented a small flat in Torquay and before the year was out Florence and Robert welcomed their first daughter, Edna.

Developments in steam and the progressive improvements in the size and speed of ships, in both the Navy and the merchant marine, led Robert to make an important decision. They needed to live where he would be better positioned to find employment. In Southampton the larger ships, mail steamers and passenger liners were making regular sailings from the busy port city, and so it seemed an obvious choice. Once again Robert was on the move and the young family arrived at James Street in the St Mary's district, only a short walk up from the docks. The districts of St Mary's, Northam and Chapel were home to thousands of men and women who worked on the ships at this time. The population had swelled from 27,000 in 1841 to 105,000 in 1900, so it had been necessary for a large area of affordable living accommodation to be developed in the form of small terraced houses set in a field grid system. They were cheap and nearly all owned by landlords: there was so much moving around in the port city that most people rented their properties. Over the coming years the Hichens family shared Nos 43 and 45, a double-fronted dwelling with six rooms, with two other families.

Robert, Florence and Edna settled into their new lives in James Street and in 1910 a second daughter, Frances, arrived. Robert was away at sea for weeks at a time serving with the Union Castle and British India Lines, travelling to places such as Norway, Sweden and St Petersburg, and while he was absent Florence did her best on the £5 per month her husband was sending home. There was no such thing as a permanent crew and on each return home Robert, like hundreds of others, had to queue up once more for a new chance of a berth and much-needed employment.

They lived in one of the busiest districts in the city, their terraced street being one of many leading off the main thoroughfare of St Mary's High Street. During the week vendors would push their carts up and down, visiting houses with their goods. Early in the morning Florence and the other women of the houses would wait outside with their jugs for the milkman to arrive and then the muffin man would come with a tray on his head, selling his buns for a couple of coppers just in time for breakfast. It must have been lonely for the women of Southampton at times and they surely looked forward to the return of their husbands, spending their days walking in the park, looking round the shops and keeping their homes clean and tidy in readiness for the day their men would come back from sea.

Returning for a short break between trips, one of the spectacles they could not fail to enjoy was a visit to the Kingsland Square Market close by at the other end of the High Street. The market had been trading in the same position for hundreds of years and when the sun went down and the paraffin lights were lit the wonderful colours, sights and smells were a welcome distraction from a life which was insecure and tough. For a penny a man would chop out a lump of salt from his huge block and further along the fishmonger would shout out his specials of crab, fresh fish and occasionally wild rabbits. There was a Punch and Judy show for the children – normally a terrifying spectacle for the younger ones – whereas the escapologist was always funny; after much huffing and puffing and straining his muscles he would leap off his chair, chains clanging in a pile at his feet. The dentist would be doing good work extracting teeth behind a curtain with a man banging a big drum in front, trying to keep time with the moans and cries of pain he was unsuccessfully attempting to hide. Then as they moved on and the cries faded, they could pause at the quack doctor's stall where an old man in a white coat preached the benefits of Beecham's remedies, the perfect aid for cleaning the liver and aiding digestion.[3]

Florence and the girls had to endure the hottest summer since records began from May all through the summer of 1911. The spring had been lovely with cloudless skies and all the children enjoying the freedom of playing outside until late in the evening, but by the end of May temperatures had risen and into June they were reaching 90°F. In their small terrace house with cramped conditions and little ventilation, it must have been unbearable. With no rain to wash into the sewer system the stench could hardly be tolerated, the fields and hedgerows became parched and the farmers began to suffer as their herds had no fresh grass to eat, which in turn meant milk prices went through the roof. At least being on the coast Florence could take Edna and Frances to the beach to paddle in the sea, but not for long; the sun shone with an intensity that burnt the skin and there was not a breath of a breeze.

Elsewhere throughout the country, as the sun beat down there was a section of society who were having a ball, literally. The rich aristocracy who made up 1 per cent of the population and who owned 60 per cent of the country were enjoying the trappings of the enormous wealth they were privileged to. In the cities there were concerts to attend, dinner parties to organise, wonderful race meetings and, of course, the coronation of George V. The motorcar had arrived too, so trips into the country or down to the sea with their perfectly prepared picnics were yet another pastime for the well-to-do. When the rich became bored of staying at home they could travel by steam train along the length and breadth of the British Isles, and when they got bored with that then on to the luxury liners they would crowd, off to visit friends, to tour Europe or across the Atlantic, bringing back with them exquisite treasures from afar. The gulf between the rich and the poor was huge and class and hierarchy meant everything to the privileged. The nemesis for the rich was on the horizon but until this happened, the poor continued to suffer.

As the summer of 1911 continued, the tide was beginning to turn, and a storm that had been brewing was about to rage, affecting many working families, especially those who made their living around the docks. The country was in the grip of a major period of unrest, one which had started in 1910. The Liberal

Government had promised a series of reforms which would improve financial, working and living conditions for all, but when other countries such as Germany and America continued to expand at a rate far outreaching Britain's capabilities, it brought the United Kingdom into a state of sharp economic decline. This led to an increasing drop in wages and escalating costs in living. Unions across the country were becoming a force to be reckoned with within each of the major industries of transport, manufacturing and shipping, so when unacceptable working conditions and poor pay became intolerable, tens of thousands of workers began to come out on strike.

In Southampton what had started out as strikes among the coal porters developed into the complete stoppage of work throughout the docks, leading to the cancellation of many Atlantic crossings. This whole situation was embarrassing for the city for two reasons. Firstly, the flagship luxury liner of the White Star Line, *Olympic*, almost didn't make its maiden voyage – due to sail to New York on 14 June and return with a whole host of millionaires – and only some fancy negotiating averted that potential calamity. Secondly, the Naval Fleet Review celebrating King George V's coronation was losing ships left right and centre because seamen were refusing to take part. The vessels, which were bedecked with their full regalia of flags and banners, were sitting idly at their berths waiting to see which way the shipping companies' thumb would turn. At the eleventh hour, or 2.10p.m. to be precise, the terms of the workers were agreed and the Review could begin.

Although the workers had won a small but significant victory, the situation for the families remained the same in Southampton and the cost of living was so high it led to grinding poverty for many. When, in January 1912, things looked as if they couldn't get any worse, they did. This time it was the turn of the coal miners to come out on strike, and without coal many liners had returned to their own ports or were tied up along the docksides in Southampton. No ships sailing meant no work for firemen, stewards, seamen, engineers and electricians; not forgetting financial worries for the scores of businesses who supplied the ships with food, clean linen, flowers and every other requirement for a long voyage.

Robert had returned from serving on the SS *Dongola*, which had been re-commissioned as a troop ship sailing the Bombay route. Now, in March 1912, with no end to the coal strike in sight and the landlord wanting his rent, the Hichens' household was in trouble. There was a small light though, at the end of a long tunnel. Another White Star Line ship was making its way from Belfast to Southampton for her maiden voyage to New York. If Robert could get to the front of the queue to sign on, with his twelve years' experience and Master Mariner's certificate, he would have as good a chance as any. The imminent arrival of the luxury liner had been causing quite a stir in the *Daily Echo*, and Quartermaster Robert Hichens was going to make quite sure he would not miss his opportunity to sail on the Royal Mail Steamer *Titanic*.

3

⇒ SETTING SAIL ⇐

Titanic was due to arrive in Southampton on the evening of 3 April. At the port a much smaller crew signed on, on Tuesday 26 March, before taking the train from West Station to Liverpool where they were to meet a steam packet that would ferry them over to Belfast to join *Titanic* and bring her down south. For this trip Master H.A. Haddock would command *Titanic* before handing over the responsibility to Captain Smith. The master was obliged 'by law' to sign and deposit a copy of the crew particulars of engagement before sailing, but on page one of the book was the following entry: 'Captain Smith was informed that he [Captain Haddock] has not signed the agreement and he has sent a message that if he could not call before he sailed he would do so on the return of the ship.' Captain Haddock had broken the law, it seemed, in not signing the crew agreement; a misdemeanour marking even the earliest stage of her journey. There were two men who appeared as quartermasters on these particulars of engagement: J. Foley and W. Weller. When they signed on again at Southampton for the voyage to New York; Foley appeared as a storekeeper and Weller as an able seaman, quite a step down from a qualified quartermaster whose role included the huge responsibility of steering the ship. George Rowe, who signed on as quartermaster in Southampton, had been a lookout on the trip down from Belfast.

Ten crewmen arrived on board *Titanic* on Good Friday, including Robert. The official signing-on day would be the following day, Saturday, when the coal strike was due to be lifted, but he had come anyway to offer his services to help dress the ship in her flags to celebrate this holy day – and as a publicity exercise. The flags had been sent down a couple of days before from Liverpool. This would be Robert's opportunity to get to know the ship a bit and admire her stunning newness. Many of the ships Robert had sailed on previously had been ropey old mail steamers and the *Dongola* troop ship, which were not a patch on this beauty.

The horse-drawn trams were not running on this religious day, so Robert no doubt enjoyed the early walk down St Mary's Street on a glorious spring morning with no one around. In a few hours, curtains would open and the kids would come tumbling out to play for a bit before returning to get dressed for Good Friday services – those whose parents bothered with the church. With so much time away at sea Robert wouldn't be able to get to regular church services, not like when he was in Newlyn.

Once he got to the dock, Robert spent a good couple of hours hoisting the bunting up and along the rigging, and *Titanic* looked splendid with the brightly coloured little banners flapping about in the breeze. Down below on the dockside a small group of photographers had gathered. They were here to capture the beauty of the new addition to the White Star Line for the weekend papers. Sitting a way up from them were two artists doing their turn at producing beautiful watercolours and oil paintings for the occasion. Four great funnels towered above Robert, for now quiet and gleaming for the artists; no clouds of black coal smoke bellowed from them as it wasn't time to fire up the boilers yet. Indeed the fourth funnel would never smoke; this was a dummy added to create the perfect complement and symmetry to the ship.

Robert spent the rest of morning and half the afternoon getting to know the parts of *Titanic* where he would be spending most of his time. The gangway entrances, bridges both fore and stern, and the standing compass between the second and third funnels up a sturdy ladder on a platform. For the hours he'd spent helping out he was due to get about 8*s* – better than nothing. Finally finished, Robert made his way down through the ship, out down one of the gangplanks reserved for crew and, with anticipation at tomorrow's official signing on, walked with a quick step back up Ocean Road towards home.

The following Saturday morning was chaos at the signing-on offices. Hundreds of men and women had been out of work for weeks and now they jostled with each other, competition fierce between the different departments that made up the huge crew for *Titanic*. Robert stood right up front with only one man ahead of him, another quartermaster, Alfred Olliver. Everyone wanted to get a berth on this fabulous new ship and much of the chatter would have been descriptions of the comfortable bunks and decent food they could expect on the voyage and which rich folk were planning to be on board. Robert was one happy man when his signature was finally on the form, with just four days to go before he could begin the most prestigious position he had held so far.

What excitement it must have been at Robert's house at 6.30a.m. Wednesday 10 April: spending his last hour with his family and enjoying a hearty breakfast before kissing them goodbye and walking down the street with Florence and the girls waving from the doorway. *Titanic* was due to arrive in New York on Wednesday 17 April and return nine days later. Robert arrived at the dock at 7.30a.m., keen to find his berth for the next two weeks. Heading to the fo'c'sle (forecastle) head he would have ducked through the hatch and down the 'glory hole' to his accommodation below. He would be sharing a dormitory with twenty-eight other men: a mixture of seamen, the boatswain, his mate, the lookouts and the other quartermasters. They would be Rowe, Bright, Humphries, Olliver and his brother-in-law Perkis and Wynn. Robert would be the only quartermaster not to have sailed with the White Star Line, as the others had been on either the *Oceanic* or *Olympic* before joining *Titanic*. None of them came from the docklands but it wouldn't be long before they got to know each other, and with Robert's usual Cornish banter and dry sense of humour, typical of Newlyn, they would no doubt get along fine. Robert and his fellow crewmen would need to get changed quickly into uniforms once on board. At 5ft 6in Robert was not a tall man, but stocky with a 40in chest. On his left arm he had a tattoo of a woman and his initials, R.H., while on his right were the Arms of Scotland and his surname, Hichens.

A whistle blew from the master at arms above and all the crew, now smartly dressed in their new White Star Line uniforms, jostled with each other to get back up on deck for 8a.m. muster. There was a buzz of anticipation as Robert took his place alongside his mates on the well deck. Every bit of deck space was filled with the more than 900 crew smartly attired in their different outfits befitting their rank and position within the ship. Captain Smith stood with his senior officers looking resplendent in their uniforms and the chief, Henry Wilde, handed the sailing report to the commander. A popular man well-liked and admired by passengers and crew, Captain Smith had been quoted with regards to his career as saying:

> When anyone asks how I can best describe my experience in nearly 40 years at sea, I merely say, uneventful. Of course there have been winter gales, storms and fog and the like but in all my experience, I have never seen a wreck, nor was I ever in any predicament that threatened to end in disaster of any sort. You see, I am not very good material for a story.[4]

There had been interesting goings-on in relation to the appointment of the officers for *Titanic*'s maiden voyage. Chief Officer Wilde, for one, hadn't expected to sail on this voyage. He didn't really like *Olympic*'s sister and he had a bad feeling about this trip. Nevertheless, Captain Smith had sailed with him previously on *Olympic* and trusted Wilde as his second in command, so when Smith had asked him to oblige, Wilde had rather grudgingly agreed. It meant that William Murdoch went from being chief to first officer. Murdoch came from a long line of Scottish seafarers. He had climbed the ladder of success very quickly and, in 1900, started his eleven-year career with the White Star Line. A competent man who made friends easily, he'd had his share of close shaves in his position as first officer while he was on *Titanic*'s sister ship, *Olympic*. She had collided with a Royal Navy vessel inflicting such serious damage an investigation was launched, and Murdoch had to defend the White Star Line. Even so, the damages awarded to the small vessel's owners almost bankrupted the shipping company. Striking a sunken wreck which lost them a propeller and almost running aground while leaving Belfast only added to the mishaps a little while later. Still, accidents happen.

A Lancashire man called Charles Herbert Lightoller was put in as second officer. He had been severely put out[5] as he had been looking forward to the rating of first officer on this important trip. A cool, ambitious man, he was waiting for the time, and hoped it would be soon, when he would become commander.

For now he would hide his bitter disappointed at the setback. David Blair had been second officer on the journey down from Belfast, but with the change in rankings he was now surplus for this one trip and he left the ship, not realising that in his pocket was jangling a very important set of keys: those to the locker in his cabin which contained the one and only pair of binoculars for the crow's nest. The other men making up the complement of officers were Third Officer Herbert Pitman, Fourth Officer Joseph Boxhall, Fifth Officer Harold Lowe and Sixth Officer James Moody. The Blue Ensign was hoisted, and Captain Smith handed over the master report to Captain Clarke of the Board of Trade who confirmed that everything was in good working order and duly signed. The whistle blew again to complete the muster and all the crew returned to their stations. In four hours *Titanic* would be ready to depart.

It was suddenly all go, and some of the quartermasters were called to man the gangplanks. In the distance could be heard the deep bellow of the Waterloo train, and then she came into view, her chocolate-brown and green paint gleaming, to deliver the second- and third-class passengers. The excitement was electric; many of the steerage passengers were leaving these shores to start their new lives in the New World. As the train came to a leisurely stop, clouds of white steam rose from her chimney and doors flew open as porters hurried along the carriages, helping the passengers down and giving out orders to get the luggage loaded on to the ship. Hundreds of expectant travellers exclaimed in awe as their eager faces lifted ever higher, not believing the sheer enormity of the leviathan they would be sailing on. Children shrieked with glee, ecstatic as their anxious parents grabbed at coat sleeves in an attempt to stop them from disappearing into the bustling crowds. All went up the gangplanks, with Robert and his mates welcoming the passengers on board and wishing them a pleasant voyage. Finally the last few, more mature guests made their way slowly, hands on rails, up the gangplanks and were welcomed into the ship's warm interior.

After 8a.m. muster and before 11a.m., some of the officers went back on shore to say their final farewells to friends and family. The managing director of the White Star Line, Bruce Ismay, was showing his family around the ship and the captain had taken the arm of his wife to guide her and their daughter around for a quick tour before it was time to leave. It was just after 11.30a.m. when once again a train's whistle blew with the arrival of the first-class passengers from London. As the locomotive advanced slowly up the tracks, a group of men could be seen hurrying from the other side, kit bags on their backs. They were two of the ship's firemen, Nutbean and Podesta, and the Slater boys who came from the Northam and Chapel area – who had just been having one last pint down the Grapes pub up from the dock. This was a favourite haunt of sailors and firemen who relished a last jar before their long voyages. Looking to the right, the men could see the train was almost upon them. Nutbean and Podesta leapt over the tracks just in time, red faced and breathing hard they hurried up the gangplank; but the Slater boys, seeing the huge metal fenders just feet from them, had left it seconds too late and could not cross. As the train steamed slowly onto its stop 100yds on, the lads ran along the other side trying to catch it up and overtake it, but again they were not quick enough. The doors opened, porters arrived and the huge amount of luggage that was essential for first-class travel was hastily taken aboard. As Robert stood by the gangplank the wealthy aristocracy wandered up, the ladies bejewelled and crowned by huge hats of ostrich feathers with all manner of exotic furs draped around their shoulders. Whispers and sighs were exchanged, some comparing this ship to that of her sister *Olympic*, twins it seemed; many had sailed in her and of course the other great liners who took them across the seas on their seemingly everlasting European and transatlantic excursions.

With everyone on board Robert at last hurried up the gangplank with his mates. Once at the top the order was given to pull the gangways in. The Slater boys now came running at top speed back down the dockside shouting and waving. They almost bundled in to the master at arms, pleading and apologising, begging to be let on – but they were too late. There were others ready to take their places on board. They had missed their chance and with the gangways finally pulled in, the doors were heaved shut. They didn't know how lucky they were to have, quite literally, missed the boat.

At one of the junior officer's command, a rope was yanked and the most mighty, deep-throated, thunderous bellow sang out across the docks and far over Southampton Water, shouting for all to hear that *Titanic* was about to set sail. Chief Officer Wilde was in charge of the moorings and the tugboat hawsers at the fo'c'sle head, and Lightoller and Murdoch were ready with their orders at the stern. With final commands ringing out, the triple-toned Stentonian whistles cried out once, twice and a final time. With his job done, Robert was free for a few minutes to look out over the Ocean Terminal building, the well-wishers frantically waving flags and shouting salutations at the tops of their voices. Every available foot of quayside was crammed with friends, relatives and Southampton residents seeing off another great liner, whose significance at the port had helped to build the prosperity of the area, even in the currently lean times. On arriving at the ship, hundreds of red rose buttonholes had been given to the gentlemen and anyone else who wanted one, and now, hanging over the rails, many of the passengers flung them back to be caught by the crowds whose arms stretched up to receive their crimson keepsakes. Florence, Edna and Frances were sure to be waving amongst the thousands of people below on such a special day. With shouts of 'be home soon; take care of yourselves', it was time for *Titanic* to leave.

High up in the bridge, Trinity House Harbour Pilot George Bowyer called 'Make fast the tugs!' Seconds later came the reply, 'Tugs all fast!' It was the pilot's responsibility to issue instructions to the quartermaster at the helm in order to perform the delicate manoeuvres needed to get this 46,000-ton ship out into the Channel and up river to open sea. This was the time the auxiliary wheel was used in the pilothouse, separate and in front of the wheelhouse. The tugs took up the slack and started to guide *Titanic* away from the quayside and into the Channel.

Over on the other side of the water, two liners were moored up together at berth No.38, out of use because of the coal strike. Indeed coal had been pirated from these and other ships along the docks to provide *Titanic* with the 6,000 tons she would need to make the journey to New York. The *Oceanic* was closest to the quayside with the liner *New York* opposite *Titanic* and the water. A small crowd of onlookers had managed somehow to gain access and had climbed over the rails of the *Oceanic*. They were now lining the rails of the *New York* and getting a cracking view of the proceedings. As *Titanic* slowly progressed towards the turning circle, the merry tunes of the Salvation Army brass band that had been playing on the quayside started to get fainter. On the port side the tugs *Neptune, Vulcan, Hercules, Albert Edward* and *Ajax* carefully pulled *Titanic* into position as they belched black smoke.

At last *Titanic*'s huge bronze propellers began to rotate, slowly to start with, then building up momentum more quickly, then faster still. A huge amount of water was gushing out, a tremendous, powerful displacement pushed out by the massive blades. On the starboard side the flow had the test river to accommodate it, but on the port side the heavy wash pushed with incredible force under and against the *Oceanic* and the *New York* on the opposite dock. The volume of water started to lift the *New York* and the crowd there gasped and clung on to the rails for grim death. The smaller liner then started to rock dangerously as *Titanic* gradually gained speed and make her way up river. As *Titanic* carried onwards, the ropes of the *New York* first became slack and then, as the ship righted itself, the pressure on the moorings increased dramatically, straining to their absolute limit.

Suddenly, there were three shrieking retorts which echoed across the water, and many onlookers made an involuntary duck for cover, the sound like loud pistol fire. The moorings had wrenched free and the ropes whipped through the air, catching one woman who was flung to the deck of the *New York*, injured. Now, with the *New York* free of her moorings she began to drift sideways across the river, sucked in towards *Titanic*. Captain Gale of the tug *Vulcan* got the call to steer in between the two ships, but this would have been suicide for the little vessel. There was no doubt that with the rate she was moving the tug would be crushed against the side of *Titanic*. Gale made an emergency decision and shouted above the melee, ordering a rope to be flung over the port quarter of the *New York*. At the first attempt the rope fell away uselessly in the water and the situation became critical. The broken mooring ropes were trailing serpent-like in the water; any minute now and they would get coiled around the tug's propellers. Gale shouted out again and another rope was thrown, this time they managed to get hold and make fast the rope to the other vessel. Gale immediately called 'Full speed ahead', and with just 4ft to spare between the *New York* and *Titanic* the little tug pulled the ship away from the brand-new gleaming hull of White Star Line's pride and joy.

Onlookers, who had stood rooted to the spot, their eyes wide and jaws open, watched as the *New York* was being sucked with so much power towards *Titanic*. It was only through the quick thinking of the *Vulcan*'s skipper and the fact that Captain Smith had ordered *Titanic*'s engines stopped that calamity had been avoided. As the *New York* was guided carefully to another berth further up river, one could almost see the ashen faces of the small crowd still gripping hold of the rail; they had chosen an unfortunate platform to watch *Titanic* leave. All those who observed the incident must have hoped it wasn't a bad omen. The crew were now heading for a complicated manoeuvre between shallow sandbanks and Calshot Spit, where only the year before *Olympic* had been steered too close to HMS *Hawke*. *Hawke* had been heading towards her with what they thought was plenty of space, but *Olympic* had sucked the ship in and a huge protruding spur at the front of the military vessel had inflicted terrible damage to *Olympic*'s hull – she had been in dry dock for three weeks for repairs This had been the collision William Murdoch had been involved in. Fortunately *Titanic* did not repeat her sister ship's mistake, and with the manoeuvre safely carried out there was nothing more for the pilot George Bowyer to do; he made his way down to the gangplank doors, which were opened for him to climb aboard the pilot vessel, and returned to harbour. Orders were given by the captain to fire up her boilers and *Titanic* was finally out in open sea and on her way to the next port, Cherbourg.

4

THE FIRST FOUR DAYS

An hour late because of the *New York* incident, *Titanic* was now moored outside Cherbourg, as she was too big for the port to accommodate her. Two hundred and seventy-four passengers had travelled down to Gare St Lazare in Paris from all over Europe. The tenders *Nomadic* and *Traffic* collected them, one to take the first-class passengers, the other to take second and third, the mail and extra luggage. Some of the more notable wealthy American passengers joining were Benjamin Guggenheim, son of a wealthy mining magnate; Isidor Straus of Macy's Department Store, and his wife; John Thayer, President of the Pennsylvanian Railroad; Major Archibald Butt, President Taft's personal aide; and John Jacob Astor IV and his second wife, Madeleine, who at nineteen was much younger than him and was expecting their first child. This couple had provided the papers with much gossip, especially as Astor was reported to be worth $150 million.

There were forty-two first-class passengers, thirty second class and 102 third class. Among them were Syrian/Armenian, Middle Eastern, Croatian and Scandinavian immigrants; indeed after English, Swedish was the second most common language spoken on *Titanic*. Robert, with two other quartermasters and four able seamen, held down the gangplanks as they alighted, ten men on each side. One woman came on board covered in fur from head to foot, a rather large lady with a loud American accent. She would later be identified as Margaret Tobin Brown, once a poor labourer's daughter of Irish descent and estranged wife of J.J. Brown, well known in Denver for striking gold at the Little Johnnie silver mine and becoming a millionaire overnight. Margaret was best described as 'new' money. She made friends easily but what she most wanted was to be accepted by the richest and noblest of her fellow ladies and gentlemen, and she had a marvellous opportunity to do this amongst the first-class passengers on *Titanic*. She never forgot her roots though and would thoroughly enjoy re-telling the story of her rise to riches in front of a polite and well-bred audience.

At 8.10p.m. *Titanic* set sail and with a glorious sunset she looked beautiful; every porthole was lit and her mast, bow stern, port and starboard lights were blazing against the spring evening on her way to Ireland. *Titanic* sailed majestically on through the night and the passengers had the opportunity to enjoy the full hospitality of this wonderful ship. First-class passengers could enjoy a swim in the heated salt-water swimming pool, or a game of tennis followed by a ride on the mechanical camel in the fully equipped gymnasium. Far less strenuous activities included sitting by the fire in the beautifully decorated reading, writing and smoking rooms, or taking a leisurely stroll around the decks. Every possibly treat and luxury was made available to the guests, some of whom had spent up to £700 for the best suites. Even the passengers in steerage were comparatively spoilt; many had been expecting to travel on other smaller liners but were transferred to *Titanic* because of the coal strike and their dining room, rest areas and sleeping accommodation were better than second class in some of the other ships.

They arrived in Queenstown, Ireland at 11.30a.m. on Thursday 11 April. Again, the harbour was not large enough to accommodate a liner the size of *Titanic* so she moored 2 miles out at Roche's Point and the tenders *America* and *Ireland* were on hand to ferry passengers and mail. Here the ship was to pick up 113 third-class passengers who, on the whole, were Irish emigrants on their way to start a new life in America, plus a handful of second-class passengers. This would be the last stop to pick up mail and 1,385 bags were hastily loaded. An hour and a half later and the *Titanic* would make her final farewell to land.

The ship was much larger than many of the crew had sailed on before and it was not just getting to know the other crew that was a challenge, but also finding their way around the labyrinth

of companionways, passages and alleys. Most of the accommodation for the crew was on E deck, below the first- and second-class
dining saloons and galley, and above the third-class dining on F
deck. The firemen and greasers were in the extreme bow on D,
F and G decks, which had a spiral staircase that led down to the
boiler rooms. On E deck were the master at arms, quartermasters, musicians, restaurant staff, stewards, seaman and a further 450
crew. Up to forty crew members could be sharing one dormitory of bunks. The mess room and galley for most of the seamen
was on C deck in the bow. Running alongside the crew accommodation on the port side of E deck was a large working alley
nicknamed 'Scotland Road'. The officers, however, called it 'Park
Lane'. There were long distances between the decks and the
'glory holes', which were where the crew accommodation was
situated, and getting lost was a common occurrence for the first
two days at sea.

One of Robert's many duties was delivering messages
throughout the ship, often down to the engineers, deep within
the bowels of *Titanic*. It was another world down there. Many
of the engineers, electricians and firemen came from the same
streets as Robert around St Mary's, Northam and Chapel.
Further down still into the great hull of the mighty liner were the
boiler and engine rooms. Here, 150 'black gang' men worked to
maintain the twenty-five double-ended triple-furnaced boilers
and four single-ended ones. *Titanic* was originally designed as a
twin-screw vessel which would mean she could achieve a speed
of 21 knots, but during construction they added a third, centre
screw, driven by a steam turbine which could increase her speed
by another 3 knots.

The black gang worked on 160 furnaces using 600 tons of coal
every day to keep the fires going; these fires heated the water in
the boilers to produce steam; the steam powered her 75,000hp
engines, and the engines drove the turbines which turned the
propellers, pushing *Titanic* ever faster towards her destination. The
black gang was the name given to all the men who managed
the fires but best described the trimmers. Theirs was the filthiest
and most physically demanding job on the ship, for which they
received the lowest rates of pay and were at the very bottom of
the crew hierarchy. At least on *Titanic* the trimmers had rather
a better time of it than some of the 'killer ships' they had sailed

on before. They were the toughest of men who, when in port for short weeks at a time, would be quick to get their pay so that they could 'let off steam' and have a few jars of rum and maybe a decent fight at one of the six pubs along Albert Road, Chapel. They would have little time to see their wives and families if they had one, but just enough to make sure their lineage continued and that they added to the growing population of the Southampton dockland. Many of the cannier wives would arrive at the shipping offices before their husbands to ensure they could get their hands on a few bob – before their greasy spouses threw the wages down their necks and disappeared for another two months until the next pay out.

On board, however, the trimmers would make sure that the huge weight of coal was distributed evenly throughout the bunkers, otherwise the ship would be likely to list. Working their hours of four on, four off, they would shovel the coal from the bunkers and, using wheelbarrows and baskets, heave their load to where the firemen (or stokers) were waiting, then drop the coal in front of each of the furnaces. Inside, the firebox was divided into two sections, top and bottom. The coal was shovelled in at the top and it would then be the turn of the firemen to make sure the fire burned evenly. If it didn't, clinkers would appear. These were hard lumps of coal or minerals that wouldn't burn, blocking the air to the fire and reducing its effectiveness. The clinkers would therefore have to be broken up using a slice bar, and would eventually fall with the other used debris into the grate below – the ash pit. The ash would in turn be removed and pumped up a pipe using high-pressure sea water, finally being shot out through a hole in the side of the ship. Even on *Titanic*, the work was not only back-breaking but searingly hot too. With only a piece of wet rag to place over their mouths and nostrils to protect them from the heat and coal dust, it is not surprising that most of these men never made it to old age.[6]

On that first night Fred Barrett, the head fireman, was working with some men on a particularly annoying problem. Not only were nearly all the boilers lit in order to keep *Titanic* steaming at almost full speed – meaning that the firemen on shift were working flat out – there was also an overenthusiastic fire burning in coal bunker No. 5. Ten men had been assigned to wet the coal and move it around to keep it under control. The pile of coal in the bunker weighed 100 tons, however, and although nothing could be seen from the surface, the fire was raging in its core. It had been fuelled by gases given off in the coal, causing it to spontaneously combust, an occurrence that although not rare was a dangerous phenomenon. Bunker No.6 next to it was also being emptied of its 100 tons to stop heat transfer. The men worked tirelessly on the fire for seventy-two hours and they finally managed to put it out by the afternoon of Saturday 13 April. Located close to the starboard bow, the heat generation had caused a weakening of the bulkhead and it was now warped. Although the captain was aware of the fire, the passengers above had no knowledge of what was raging deep beneath their feet.

Supervising and working with these men on an ordinary day were the engineers. They made sure the greasers, firemen and trimmers worked with the efficiency that Chief Engineer Joseph Bell expected of them. Being such a tough and raucous lot, they had to be handled in a certain way: not too heavy or they became mutinous; too soft and the work would not progress. The crew-men who operated the boilers and engine equipment included twenty-four engineers, six electrical engineers, two boilermakers and a plumber and his clerk. The senior engineers had the job of managing the black gang and all had duties looking after the reciprocating engines, turbine and other machinery. The steering gear, pumps, refrigeration and entire electrical requirements for the ship were operated from here. As it would turn out for the men working tirelessly beneath the luxury and calm of the upper decks, their determination, bravery and unfailing work ethic to get the job done would very soon become their epitaph; not one of these brave and highly skilled men would survive the calamity that was just hours away.

The outer bridge housed the auxiliary wheel (used for pilot-ing the ship in and out of harbour), three engine telegraphs, the watertight door indicators and a number of telephones. Open wings on either side of the enclosed pilothouse provided the means by which the officer on watch could survey the sea with their powerful binoculars. By far the most important responsibil-ity Robert and the other quartermasters held was as helmsman in the wheelhouse. Many of the harbours had been built for much smaller vessels so the job of manoeuvring ships the size of *Titanic* in and out of port was often extremely tricky, and managed under the watchful eye of the harbour pilot. The quartermasters would take intricate instructions from these expert master mariners but it would be the helmsman at the wheel who ultimately steered the ship. For this reason the quartermasters were considered highly trained and valuable members of the crew and were held in high regard by their officers. In the time Robert had spent at the helm of *Titanic* since they left Southampton, he had become adept at maintaining an even keel and understanding with a keen sense how she would respond to each change of course and every type of weather condition they might expect on route. For her maiden voyage the sea had so far been calm and the conditions favourable.

In 1912 the steering orders were always given in relation to the tiller. To go to port, the officer ordered starboard. The wheel would then be turned to port, the tiller would go to starboard and the ship would turn to port. Robert took all his navigational orders from the officers on the bridge. Once given the order, he would then repeat it back to the officer to demonstrate the command had been heard and understood. The quartermasters were highly trained in navigation and keeping the logbooks up to date, and at his post at the wheel Robert could at any time relay the important information to the officers from his course board – correct time, compass readings and commutator (or clinom-eter, which in 1912 was the word used to describe the equipment that read the list of the ship). He would also operate the standing compass on the platform mid-ship where large course changes would be executed, and keep the lights trimmed there whenever it was needed. Operating the bridge bell was another function all the quartermasters performed, ringing the bell to indicate the time in half hour or hourly intervals and also fifteen minutes before a change of shift was due.

Robert's official title was quartermaster, however he could also be called petty officer, third mate, warrant officer or junior officer. It was the case on *Titanic* that all the lower-ranking seamen were called able seamen, unlike other vessels where they might have the title of 'ordinary' or 'leading' seamen. This came into play as the trade unions were developed and new rates of pay were introduced for different ranking crewmen. *Titanic* was designed in such a way as to ensure that these lower-ranking crew did not have to come into contact with the passengers. Only the likes of stewards, maids, bellboys, boots and restaurant staff had any direct contact with them. They were appointed and trained to a high standard and knew exactly how to behave and tend to the passengers' needs. The ship was divided up so that the majority of the crew scurried about their daily routines behind the mahogany-panelled walls and beneath the lush, red, thick carpets without ever being seen by the passengers.

Conditions that evening seemed normal, but it had been an unusual winter in the north Atlantic. The Hydrographic Office had reported that air and sea temperatures had risen to above average, and as a result a great many more icebergs had broken off (or calved) from the Arctic Circle and Greenland's massive coast of ice. This ice drifted down on the Labrador current off the Grand Banks of Newfoundland, and many ships reported seeing ice days before *Titanic* would be anywhere near the region. Captain Smith was made aware of some of these reports, which he had been heard to comment were not unusual for April. The ice consisted of mountainous, gleaming white bergs up to 300ft tall and twice as wide. Smaller bergs of 50ft were also common and the most treacherous. Along with the icebergs was field ice, which stretched for miles around and could easily trap ships for days as they struggled to find a passage out to safer waters. By the end of March, scores of ships were reporting their sightings of ice on an almost daily basis, and several near misses were relayed when the ships reached port (not all vessels had the luxury of wireless communication).

On 8 April the British steamer *Royal Edward* had flashed a warning of thick ice, heavy loose field ice and an iceberg. An 86-ton schooner called *Blue Jacket* had encountered huge gales and field ice, too; at the end of March with ice surrounding her close to the coast of Newfoundland, she was buffeted again by storms and so much ice that it threatened to crush her sides. She was holed and close to sinking when the vessel *Samara* came to her rescue. Ships of all sizes and types were passing ice in every direction, some struggling through successfully, others so badly damaged they had to flee to the nearest port or wait for help to arrive. On 11 April the French ship *Niagra*, close to the track *Titanic* would be taking, reported that they had passed thirty large icebergs and extensive field ice; some bergs being 400ft high and ice packs ¼–½ mile in length. *Niagra* received some damage from the pressure of the ice grinding along her side, with plates buckling below the water line, and although water had come in, the crew were able to make repairs and she slowly proceeded to port.[7]

Sunday morning, 14 April, and in the chart room one solitary ice report was plotted to the far north of the route *Titanic* was taking. It had come in through the wireless room from the French vessel *La Touraine* and been delivered to the bridge. At 10.30a.m. Captain Smith was taking Divine Service in the first-class dining saloon for all classes of passengers. Robert and the other quartermasters, lookouts and seamen had expected to muster for lifeboat drill at this time, but there would be no lifeboat drill since leaving Southampton. Situated behind the officers' quarters on A deck was the small wireless room. Here the two operators, Harold Bride and his senior, Jack Phillips, worked flat out on the large number of messages that were being sent through the new Marconi wireless system. With a range of up to 1,000 miles, the passengers, especially first class who could afford to pay the 3s for the privilege, could spend many a happy hour in one of the salons or in their cabins writing to friends and loved ones on other ships or at home, and the wireless room was becoming bombarded. Employed and paid by Marconi, Bride and Phillips operated on a piece-work basis, so the more messages they could send from passengers, the more money they earned. They were, however, also responsible for making sure messages from other ships were relayed to the officers on the bridge. A message would need to be prefixed with 'MSG' in order for it to be deemed important enough to get to the bridge. Both men were known to be under enormous pressure and Phillips was also up to his eyes with doing the accounts.

Reports showed that at 1.42p.m. a message from the ship *Baltic*, returning from New York to Liverpool, came through the wireless room. She reported large quantities of ice in latitude 41° 51' N, longitude 49° 52' W and added her best wishes for *Titanic*'s successful passage. The message was delivered to Captain Smith but it was only put on the chart room notice board at 7.15p.m. because it had spent the afternoon first in the pocket of the captain, and then in the pocket of managing director of the White Star Line, Bruce Ismay. At 1.45p.m. another message was relayed from the liner *Amerika*, reporting passing two icebergs in the region. As the message was not prefixed with 'MSG', however, it did not get delivered and was filed with all the other 'dealt with' messages. At 7.30p.m. the *Californian* sent a message warning of three large icebergs in the vicinity. Bride later reported he took the message to the bridge and gave it to one of the officers, but he didn't know which.

The temperature had dropped significantly since 6p.m. when he was last outside, so Robert would have been grateful for the hot meal inside him before heading up the 'glory hole', through the fo'c'sle head hatch, and on up to the bridge and the wheel-house for his shift.

5

'ICE, RIGHT AHEAD!'

Robert came on duty and struck eight bells, signalling it was time for the junior officers to change shift. As Pitman handed over to Boxhall, he said, 'Here's a bunch of sights for you old man', giving him a set of charts he and Lightoller had been working on earlier that evening.[8] Robert's first task was to go below deck with a message for the carpenter whose responsibility it was to look after the fresh water supplies. Robert warned him to beware, as with the drop in temperature they were likely to freeze. He added the order to pass the word on to the engine room for them to take care of the steam winches. Robert's watch this evening was from 8p.m.–12a.m. The first two hours of the shift were to be spent as standby for Quartermaster Olliver, who was at the wheel. Robert's duties would be to answer to the needs of the officers, run errands and take messages until it was his turn at the wheel at 10p.m.

Captain Smith had been dining with the Wideners in the first class à la carte restaurant. Mr Widener was heir to one of the largest fortunes in Philadelphia, his father a prominent member of the Fidelity Trust Company, the bank that controlled International Mercantile Marine, and so the trust of the White Star Line. The lavish banquet was being held in honour of the captain's upcoming retirement, having served thirty years with the shipping company. The Wideners had enjoyed sailing with him many times and they had a high regard for their friend. Further guests included some of the wealthiest first-class passengers, as well as the US President's personal aide, Colonel Archibald Butt. Smith enjoyed a sumptuous dinner, finishing with the best of Cuban cigars. He had refused the fine wines and champagne, however. As captain, alcohol was forbidden to him, even on this special occasion.

Making his deliberations, the captain arrived on the bridge just after 9p.m. and sought out Lightoller, who was now in his position out on the bridge looking through his powerful binoculars at the expanse of ocean. For the senior officers on duty on the outer bridge the responsibility was huge and although they had lookouts for support, ultimately it remained the job of the bridge officer to identify any obstructions or hazards ahead. They spoke for a while and, taking one more look at the stars settling on the horizon, he left Lightoller to join Boxhall in the chart room at the rear of the wheelhouse. Here they could be seen pouring over the charts, calculating the stellar readings and positions of ice which were showing far north of the track the ship was taking. They were not due to reach the ice region for another hour. Noting the positions on the chart, Captain Smith was seen leaving to turn in for a rest – but never far away from his bridge.

Lightoller called Moody over to him and instructed the sixth officer to telephone through to the crow's nest to alert Jewell and Symons to keep a sharp lookout for ice, especially small ice and growlers. The larger icebergs were easy to see; much more hazardous were the growlers which were low lying on the surface, carried eight-tenths of their deadly cargo beneath sea level, and were particularly treacherous for ships. They were also instructed to pass on the message to all the lookouts until daylight.

Robert went out to the cold boat deck to take the water temperature, but he was struggling. The leather scoop attached to a 20-fathom line was missing and in its place was a device which had been fashioned from an old paint can attached to a rope with a piece of twisted wire. Robert slung the rope over the rail but the can could barely reach the water; the length of rope was on the short side and the calm, flat sea didn't help. He did the best he could with the water he salvaged, took the reading from the mercury and returned to the wheelhouse to put the reading in the logbook, as was his duty; it was not his place to question the absence of proper nautical equipment. The night before, a sailor had been spotted by first-class passenger Mahala Douglas not even bothering with the task and actually filling the can with water from a tap to use for his reading. The air and water temperatures were, however, considered an essential guide as to the proximity of ice by most conscientious seafarers, and they would be taken every two hours.

Robert had experience of ice and had seen it on his voyages in the far north Atlantic. As such he must have been keenly aware how much the temperature had dropped since his earlier watch, and been glad to return from the bitterly cold deck. It had been reported, in fact, that the temperature had dropped 10°F altogether in just three hours. Before Lightoller had gone outside for his watch he had told Robert to get the heaters fired up in the officers' section and bridge area. Although hardly warm, the wheelhouse was a welcome respite and the quartermaster stood by his mate Olliver waiting for orders. Robert checked the compass, which read 'north 71 west', then the course board, noting that the ship was travelling at 22.5 knots. As the tenth hour drew near another officer would come to relieve Lightoller on the outer bridge – although at this point Robert did not know who it would be. He would not have long to mark time before it would be his time to change job too, for at 10p.m. Robert was put in charge of the wheel.

Frederick Fleet and Reginald Lee took over the watch from Archie Jewell and Alfred Symons in the crow's nest at 10p.m. They received the message to watch out for small ice and left for the warmth of the decks below. At twenty-four, Fleet was the younger of the two. This would be his second position as a lookout with the White Star Line, having served four years on the *Oceanic*. Lee was the older and more experienced man at forty-one. He'd gone to sea at sixteen, spending most of his career with the Royal Navy. He'd also been lookout on the SS *Minnehaha* and his last post had been on the *Olympic*. As they settled into their watch, Lee and Fleet felt the temperature drop considerably; so much so that Lee telephoned to the bridge that he could 'smell' ice. This in itself should have been a clear indication to the officer on watch that extra care was needed.

The lookouts' only protection from the bitter cold was a canvas screen behind them. To add to their plight, they would have to watch without their binoculars tonight. Although each officer on the bridge had binoculars, the lookouts in the nest for this trip had been without any since leaving Southampton. They'd had them when they left Belfast but Officer Bailey had locked them in his locker before leaving the ship at Southampton, and had walked off with the key. Although the lookouts had asked for some, they still hadn't been given any; a bone of contention during the lookouts' discussions in the mess. But no matter tonight, the visibility was good and they had to get on regardless. So taking their positions, Fleet on the left and Lee on the right, 40ft up the foremast, they dutifully scanned the horizon and all around. This would be their billet for the next two hours or so, and although freezing, the next hour and a quarter would pass uneventfully – until 11.15p.m.

Throughout the ship those not already asleep were bedding down for the night. Most of the public areas had already closed, while in the first-class smoking room a solitary card game was still in progress and a small group of Canadian gentlemen were enjoying a night cap and a final game of bridge. The band was playing their final set for the night, soft melodies drifting through the smoky haze. In steerage, the lights had been extinguished an hour before, encouraging the third-class passengers to head for their cabins. With Sunday being a religious day and the temperature having taken a drastic fall during the evening, *Titanic*'s passengers and off-duty crew were more than happy to slip into the comfort of their warm beds. The decks outside were almost completely deserted, far too cold to be enjoyed. Quartermaster Harold Rowe was stamping his feet far aft of the ship on the poop deck, checking his watch to see how much longer he would have before he could leave his freezing post. The other on-duty seamen were below, hanging about and waiting for any unlikely orders at this time of night. They weren't required to scrub decks as it was a Sunday, and some were gathered chatting in and around their mess hall. Even though they were heading towards the ice region, Lee and Fleet remained the only lookouts in the crow's nest on duty, and on deck there was just one seaman patrolling the decks.

Luis Klein, a Hungarian who spoke little English, had worked for the Austro-American Line before signing up on *Titanic* in Liverpool; now, on this cold, clear night, he shoved his hands deep in his pockets, pulled up his coat collar and headed towards the bow. As he was passing the officers' quarters on the starboard side he could hear laughter and merriment coming from one of the cabins, and was greatly surprised to see a number of senior crew members enjoying what looked like wine or champagne, with stewards serving them their drinks.[9] Meanwhile, Robert stood at the helm, bathed in a soft glow from the lamps on his course board, which had been trimmed earlier. After dark all the blinds had been closed in the wheelhouse so that no light would escape to the outer bridge and hinder the night vision for the officer on watch. For now he was alone: Boxhall had left the chart room shortly after the captain, saying he was going for a tea break; his mate Olliver was trimming the lights on the standard compass, up on a platform between the second and third funnels amid ship; and Sixth Officer Moody had left on some errand and informed Robert that he would return shortly.[10]

Up in the crow's nest, the glacial night was as much as the two lookouts could bear. Stamping their feet and blowing clouds of breath, ice started to form on their eyelashes and brows. Pummelling their arms and clapping their gloved hands together would be the best they could do in an effort to stop them going numb with cold. Their warm woollen hats and extra pullovers beneath their coats at least gave them some comfort as the temperature ducked to below freezing. Now, at 11.15p.m., they spotted the first ominous black outline appearing over the horizon. Lee had been around ice before up near this region and recognised the need to signal to the bridge: the first bell was rung.[11] There was no response, but they must have been confident the officer on watch would have seen the berg through his binoculars. Far enough away not to be a danger, the course remained the same and *Titanic* sailed on. After a few minutes, more ice came into view; they were now definitely heading towards the reported ice region. A dark shape was clearly silhouetted against the starry sky, and the lookouts rang the bell for a second time. Fleet then rang the bridge, but no answer came. The lookouts waited for *Titanic* to alter course or slow down in response, but instead they sped ahead with no change at all.[12]

From his position Robert would have been able to hear the crow's nest's bell clearly, breaking the silence in the wheelhouse, and the lookouts calling 'ice ahead'. A few minutes passed and the bell rang again, and this time the telephone behind him rang too.[13] Moody had said he would be back soon, but Robert was surely beginning to wonder what was going on; hadn't the officer on watch heard the lookouts? And if he had, why wasn't he responding? Robert, however, could do nothing without further information but hold the wheel steady. It was not his position to call out, and it was unthinkable for him to leave the wheel – so he continued to keep *Titanic* on her course. Robert wasn't the only man to have heard the lookouts, however. Fireman Jack Podesta and his mate William Nutbean had been finishing their meal in the mess hall, which was close to the well deck. As they were heading for their quarters they heard a man in the crow's nest shouting 'ice ahead'. They went out on deck to look around but they saw nothing except the calm, pitch-black night; their eyes unaccustomed due to the bright interior they had come from. Shrugging at each other, they went back in to their bunks below.

In the wheelhouse, Robert listened as the men up in the crow's nest tried to attract the attention of the bridge. The bell rang once more. Where was the officer on watch? Robert would have known they were due to reach the reported ice region off the banks of Newfoundland soon, but his position dictated he could not leave his post. Indeed this would have been the worst breech of discipline. The situation would have clearly been causing him concern; he at least knew warnings were not being heeded. At 22.5 knots, almost full speed, Robert would certainly have asked himself what the hell this 46,000-ton liner was sailing into.

Fleet and Lee must have been getting very worried, too. They had seen ice twice, reported it three times, and were heading for treacherous waters with no change in course or reduction of speed and no affirmation from the bridge – why? This had the potential to be an emergency on the grandest scale, but without a response from the bridge they were rendered helpless. As another berg came into view, small at first then getting larger as it headed directly for them, their fears began to be realised.

Robert would now have to make a desperate decision. He needed to find out why the officer on watch was not responding to the calls from the crow's nest, and the only way he could do this was to leave his post, alone as he was at the wheel. He would have to run a few steps to reach the bridge. Deciding there was no choice, he wrenched himself away from the wheel and ran outside. There was no one on the outer bridge but, at the rear of the pilothouse, lying prostrate on a bench, was a man dressed in an overcoat and scarf wearing the uniform of an officer. God only knows how this sight must have appeared to Robert; all he could do was to try to wake the officer up by shouting in his ear – but the prone figure didn't move.[14] It was no use, Robert sprinted back to his position at the wheel and held the course which at least hadn't altered.

Fleet and Lee weren't the only men to have seen the final iceberg; the Hungarian seaman at the bow, Luis Klein, had seen it too. Klein shouted a warning and rushed towards the bridge. He too saw the officer asleep on the bench, and he flew onwards to where he had previously seen the other men enjoying themselves, almost colliding with Third Officer Pitman on the way.[15] Robert, back at his post, heard quick footsteps approach and Sixth Officer Moody came into the wheelhouse. Suddenly there were three loud gongs from the crow's nest and the call 'Ice, right ahead!', then the telephone peeled into life. Moody grabbed the receiver: 'What do you see?' On hearing the answer he slammed the phone down, shouting himself, 'Ice, right ahead!' Murdoch's Scottish accent would next be heard shouting from the bridge outside: 'Hard-a-starboard!' In response, Robert immediately threw his whole weight behind the wheel, feet anchored to the ground, spinning it all the way to the left and repeating 'Hard-a-starboard, the helm is hard over!' The engine telegraph rang and painfully slow seconds later another order sang out in an attempt to pull the stern away from the berg: 'Hard-a-port!'[16] Just moments later the most sickening of grinding sounds and a vibration from the bottom of the ship confirmed only one thing – they had hit. Robert then heard another bell ring; the one that instructed the engine room to close the watertight doors.

In the crow's nest Fleet and Lee could only stare transfixed, backing away into the canvas behind them as if the flimsy material would give them protection from the icy assailant that was heading towards them. The telephone receiver was swinging off the hook behind them; they had finally got their response from the bridge. Fleet tried to persuade Lee to save himself and pushed him towards the ladder. Lee turned and dropped through the hatch, making to climb down and away from this nightmare, but he couldn't leave Fleet whatever happened, and with no further thought he pulled himself up back to his position.[17] The men prepared to meet their maker. The ice came closer and closer still but it looked as though it was slightly off the starboard bow and yes, maybe, they were going to just miss it. The ice passed impossibly close to the side of the ship and Lee turned and muttered to his mate, 'That was a narrow shave'.[18] Suddenly they felt and heard an ominous grinding as the ship crushed the ice and some of it scraped off and fell on to the well deck as the berg disappeared from view. Far aft Quartermaster Rowe saw what he thought looked like the sails of a windjammer coasting past in the night. Fourth Officer Boxhall felt the vibration too and ran to the bridge just in time to hear Murdoch give the 'Hard-a-port' order.[19]

Captain Smith rushed to the bridge. The entire event had taken no more than a few minutes. 'What have we hit?' he demanded. The first officer replied, 'An iceberg. I tried to port round it but it was too close and we hit.' 'Close the watertight doors,' came the response.[20] Robert could see nothing, but could hear the men from his post: 'They are already closed,' the officer replied. Ominously, as Robert looked over to the commutator he could already see the ship was listing at a 5° angle on the starboard side.

Passengers and crew throughout the ship became aware of the impact, but only slightly: some later reported that the feeling was like running over a thousand marbles; a chain passing over an anchor; or the sound of calico ripping with just the faintest of vibrations. By now the other officers had arrived at the bridge and within minutes the ship's designer Thomas Andrews and Bruce Ismay, managing director of the White Star Line, joined them, crowding the wheelhouse. As the seriousness of the situation became clearer, Captain Smith ordered the carpenter to be sent for to sound the ship. Thomas Andrews went below to make a damage report and Boxhall was sent to the wireless room to order the operators Bride and Phillips to call for help and give *Titanic's* position. Robert was to stay at his post until the time he was due to be relieved, 12.25a.m. Captain Smith needed to know in detail what had happened and he led the men out to the bridge. Now only able to hear muffled voices, one can only speculate at this point what must have been going through Robert's head: he had been steering *Titanic* when she hit the ice, would he be blamed for the catastrophe? Would anyone want to sail with him again? Sailors were very superstitious men – would they think he was jinxed? Robert was ultimately only a quartermaster; his actions and what he had witnessed had put his entire future in jeopardy.

Boxhall soon returned to report he had seen water in the mail-room. At 12.25a.m., Thomas Andrews returned to the bridge to give the captain his damage report. Notably, this was forty-five minutes after *Titanic* had first struck the iceberg. With his report completed, the outcome was finally clear. The ice had punctured a number of holes along the starboard bow from boilers Nos 6 to 2, and the water was pouring in at such a rate that the compartments were filling rapidly. The ship could survive with two compartments filled, but as soon as water breached the fifth compartment the weight would cause *Titanic* to tip uncontrollably and, in what Andrews estimated to be one to one and a half hours, the ship would sink. 'There must be no panic,' declared Captain Smith. 'Uncover the boats and take out the tackle. Women and children first.'

On Sunday 14 April 1912, between 11.40p.m. and 12.25a.m., Captain Smith, his senior officers, Thomas Andrews and Bruce Ismay would have been in deep consultation about the events that had just taken place. They had a forty-five-minute timespan in which to discuss the preceding events. Did they in this time also decide what information should be shared and, more importantly, what information should be kept silent? At this point, nobody on *Titanic* knew who would live and who would die. It seems extraordinary that Charles Lightoller, not on duty at the time of the collision and normally holding the senior rank of first officer, and the owner of the ship, Bruce Ismay, should be the ones destined to survive. It would be five days later in a chandeliered senate room in New York before anyone would come close to discovering the answer to this question and many others in a drama laid out for the world to see. Back on *Titanic*, forty-five minutes after they had been hit, the harrowing events of the next few hours continued to unfold.[21]

6

═══╬═ LIFEBOAT 6 ═╬═══

Deep in the bowels of the ship, Chief Fireman Fred Barret was barking orders and the men of the black gang were running in every direction. As soon as the watertight doors had been closed, the dampers of all furnaces were dropped and the men set to work putting out the fires. The enormous pressure of the engines stopping and the valves being shut sent powerful steam shooting up and out of the ventilation pipes at the front of each forward funnel, and the sound was deafening. Pumps were being hauled into place as they desperately attempted to reduce the water pouring in at an alarming rate.

Messages had been sent down to the stewards on each deck and now they were knocking on all the cabin doors. Passengers were instructed to wear warm clothing, put on their life jackets and calmly make their way up on deck, just as a precaution. The atmosphere appeared orderly, with people feeling more irritated at having been disturbed than worried.

Margaret Tobin Brown, in one of the E deck's state rooms, had popped her head out of her door to see what all the fuss was about and was assured that she really must go up on deck. She returned to layer herself with furs, extra coats, six pairs of stockings and a huge hat. Finally donning her lifejacket, she left her cabin and followed in the wake of the upper class and well bred, no doubt offering assistance to them if they were in need.[22]

Quigg Baxter knocked on the door of his mother's stateroom, B58/60. The decadent and beautiful suite was surpassed only by the one opposite, which had been occupied by Bruce Ismay. Hélène Baxter had been suffering with terrible seasickness throughout the journey, and was in the throes of a panic attack. Quigg's father, James 'diamond' Baxter, had been a hugely successful jewellery maker and had opened up Montreal's first shopping complex before creating his own private bank; one of Canada's largest. When he embezzled it out of $40,000 he was found out and sent to jail; he died not long after his release. On this Atlantic voyage, Quigg had joined his mother and his sister Suzette on a tour of Europe, with his rather flamboyant mistress and courtesan, Berthe Maine, in tow. She had been a cabaret singer in Belgium and on this trip she was subtly accommodated in a first-class cabin, one deck below. During this voyage she would be known as Madame de Villiers so as not to draw attention to her rather exotic alter ego. Now at his mother's door, Quigg helped Hélène from the cabin and had to half carry her up on to deck where she could rest. He took out a small silver flask of brandy from his coat pocket and placed it in his mother's hand.

In first-class cabin C104, Major Arthur Peuchen was trying to decide whether to take his $200,000 in bonds and $100,000 in stocks as he dressed himself in two sets of long underwear and his tailored, heavy winter suit and overcoat. He chose instead to reach for his small yacht master's pin, which he fastened it to his collar; closing the tin containing the bonds and grabbing a couple of oranges he left his cabin for the boat deck.

Mrs Lucien Smith, daughter of Virginian congressman Anthony Hughes, was likewise deliberating over what to carry with her, and chose to return to her cabin for her precious jewels. She was stopped, however, by her dashing young husband and was told not to worry about such trifles. Lucien helped his wife of only a few months with her warm clothing and together they followed their fellow passengers.

Edith Bowerman, a militant feminist, was travelling on *Titanic* with her daughter Elise to visit friends in Ohio. Both women were heavily involved in the more extreme practices of the Suffrage Movement, which had gotten them arrested and injured during some of the more violent protests they attended to promote women's rights. Now huddled together on deck, mother and daughter were waiting for the lifeboats to be made ready.

Soon they were joined by the Baxters, Margaret Tobin Brown, the Smiths and an attractive middle-aged lady, Helen Churchill Candee, on the arm of Colonel Archibald Gracie, a tall, striking man with a handlebar moustache who was taking a very keen interest in Mrs Candee's well-being. He was one of the members of a social group that had been established on the trip called 'Our Coterie'. Helen Churchill Candee, another staunch feminist, had previously fled from her abusive husband. A celebrated writer on interior design, she had been touring Europe alone, and was now returning to New York where her son had been injured in an automobile accident. At the top of the social hierarchy, she was to boast President Taft and the Roosevelts as some of her closest friends. She hadn't been in short supply of companions on this trip either, with many men eager to attend to her every need.

Major Peuchen then arrived and stood next to Mrs Candee. They heard a commotion and, glancing towards one of the hatches, saw a large group of sooty firemen with their kit bags slung over their shoulders, ready to leave on a lifeboat and escape from the chaos down below. Chief Officer Wilde shouted at the men, giving orders over the din of the steam, and they turned reluctantly to go back to where they had come from. Peuchen exclaimed, 'How marvellous! What an excellent example of discipline from that fine officer.'[23] Mrs Candee was not so impressed; she was worried for the poor men. Neither was to know, however, that Wilde had sent the men to their certain deaths.

Before the officers had left for their lifeboat stations, Captain Smith had called them into an office. From a locked cupboard he produced a package and, unwrapping its heavy cloth, he revealed a number of brand-new shining revolvers. After loading the guns he handed them out to each officer, should they be needed if there was a rush for the boats. Officer Lowe did not need one – he had his own. The officers left and continued to their positions to supervise the lifeboats; twenty all told, which had enough room for precisely one-third of *Titanic*'s passengers.

Robert, after finally being relieved from his post, left the wheelhouse and went to the boat deck. As he did so he was confronted with the thunderous sound of the steam, which would have made it impossible to hear himself think clearly – probably a blessing after what he had just witnessed. He then walked briskly to one of the emergency boats, which was his station when he was on duty. There had been no formal boat drill since joining *Titanic* at Southampton, which many of the crew thought peculiar; the one planned for earlier in the day had been replaced by Divine Service. He had only been to a 6p.m. muster each night for the emergency boats, in the event such as a man overboard. His only station while on duty was for that on the emergency boats and he had seen no list telling crew where they should be if there was an incident. In the event, Robert rushed up on deck to the first-class promenade. He had just taken off the covers and grips from one of the collapsible boats when he was ordered by Lightoller to a boat on the port side.

Lifeboat 6 was the second boat from forward and had already been swung out, covers off and sails and mast removed to make more room for passengers. 'Women and children first' came the direct order from Captain Smith, with Lightoller repeating the command. As Robert jumped into the boat to make ready to leave the stricken ship, Fleet was hastily encouraging the group including the Baxter family and Mrs Candee over the rail and on board. Some of the ladies had other ideas about leaving the safety of the luxury liner; there would later be many heart-breaking and well-documented accounts of women refusing to leave their husbands. Mrs Lucien Smith clung to her husband, but he gently pulled her from him and asked her, for this one and only time, to obey him and get in the boat. Composing herself, she obliged. Mrs Leila Meyer, wife of a well-known New York merchant, had been on her way home for her father's funeral; her husband practically threw her into the boat. She would lose two men she loved on this voyage. Quigg helped his mother over the side and into the boat, but not before his mistress Berthe, perhaps aware that she may not see him again, rushed over pleading hysterically with him in French, only to be prised away and put in the boat next to the other women. Margaret had made off to encourage some of the other ladies to do as they were told, but as she passed by lifeboat 6 she was grabbed by an officer and manhandled in. Mrs Candee began to board, but as she climbed in she fell awkwardly, landing on an oar and twisting her ankle at such an angle that it fractured, causing her to collapse in pain.

As more women climbed into the boat, Robert glanced around to see how many were on board and came face to face with two small, shining eyes and a furry face. A tiny Pomeranian lapdog peered out from the coat collar of Mrs Rothschild, wife of a New York Jewish clothing manufacturer, who was trying to find room in which to sit. Seaman Hemmings, who should have made up the crew of the lifeboat, had climbed out to help another sailor with the falls as, being new, they kept sticking. The scene was organised, albeit with the thunderous blowing off of steam, but suddenly it stopped abruptly and when it did the silence was profound.[24]

More anxious women had been added to Robert's boat, and now with twenty-eight on board it seemed that no more were going to get in. Lightoller gave the order to 'lower the boat away' and a trimmer passed quickly by, handing Robert a lamp. They were lucky; many of the lifeboats had no lamps and none had compasses. As their lifeboats were lowered the captain and Lightoller gave firm instructions for the men commanding them to head for a vessel they had seen earlier which looked like a steamer, two points on the port bow and about 5 miles distance. Most of the crew heading off in their boats could see this white light, which appeared on the horizon. Robert was ordered to offload the passengers at that vessel then return to the ship; this was a direct order and Robert called up his affirmation. He took one more look up to the retreating deck and saw rockets being fired high up into the sky to call for other ships to come to the rescue. He would also have seen the faces of husbands and fathers smiling and waving reassuringly to their loved ones, in total ignorance of their coming fate. How many of them would live to see their families again?

The mortally wounded *Titanic* was now listing further, making it difficult to lower lifeboats on the port side. Using oars and their hands to push away, Robert's boat began its slow descent. It started to drop at a precarious angle, frightening his passengers, and Robert called up to 'steady forward' and lower away a bit more astern. It was at this point he realised there was only him and one other seaman, nowhere near enough to man the 30ft, heavy wooden lifeboat filled with passengers. In reality he needed at least another three crew to man the oars, and if the wind picked up a little, they would be in trouble. In a fair wind the boat would be highly likely to capsize. Robert called up to *Titanic*'s deck that he only had one crew member, but could not be sure if anyone had heard him.

As the lifeboat was almost at water level, Robert looked up to see a man shimmying down the rope. Landing in front of him he asked, 'What do you want me to do?' The man puffed himself up and made himself look very important, and Robert supposed an officer must have sent him down. He wasn't part of the crew but looked from first class. He was to learn much later that this man was Arthur Peuchen, manufacturer of chemicals, a major in the Canadian Militia and a keen yachtsman. Robert didn't know him from Adam. 'Get down and put that plug in,' Robert ordered. Many of the lifeboats had problems with getting the plugs in with the number of passengers, life belts getting in the way, plus all the confusion. This had led to some of the boats carrying water halfway up to people's knees and some survivors suffered horrendous, freezing feet. After a while, the major appeared again, unable to locate the plug, so swapping places, Robert headed for the bowels of the boat and the major came forward to free the shackles.

Finally lifeboat 6 hit the water. There was no time for conviviality; back at the tiller Robert knew what a dangerous predicament they were in and what a huge responsibility lay before him. He shouted, 'Hurry up, this boat is going to founder'. The major thought he meant the lifeboat, when in fact Robert was referring to *Titanic*. The ship was gradually going by the head and the occupants of the lifeboat were understandably in a bad condition and very upset. There was nothing for it, however; they had to get away from the side of the ship as fast as they could. This 46,000-ton liner would create such a massive suction she would pull everything down with her. It had only been four days since the *New York* nearly collided with *Titanic* as it was sucked towards it in Southampton. Hundreds had seen it happen, and it was an image Robert was sure to remember very clearly.

Robert instructed them to man the oars, ladies and all: 'All of you, do your best,' he called to the fearful passengers. Fleet and the major sat at the bow of the lifeboat, each with an oar, and began to frantically row away from the looming disaster as fast as they could. Margaret Brown grabbed an oar and shouted to two other ladies to do the same. 'That's it, now row like galley slaves,' she boomed. The two galley slaves in question were Mabel and Ruth, cashiers from one of the restaurants. Robert could only look ahead as he was concentrating on steering the boat towards the light far away in the distance.

Lifeboat 6 was now widely spaced among four other lifeboats, all heading for the same light. Not ten minutes into the rowing, however, and the major began demanding that he should swap places with Robert. He wanted to be at the tiller whilst Robert rowed, but the quartermaster was having none of it. He knew that if an officer was not there to man a lifeboat it would always fall to the quartermaster or seaman to take the role. Robert had been given direct orders to command this lifeboat from his senior officers and nothing would move him from his position. 'I am put here in charge of this boat,' he shouted. 'Go and do what you are told to do.' The women in the boat would later berate the major for his pompous attitude – but Peuchen would not forget Robert's rebuff when he later testified at the Inquiry. It was a brooding and sullen man who took up his oar next to Fleet once more. At this point, a final passenger was to make his debut. Out from deep beneath the bowels of the lifeboat, underneath the seats, crawled a young stowaway of Latin appearance with an injured arm. He might now make up a scratch crew of four, but when he tried to take an oar it was obvious that he would be of no use with his disability and he was kept out of the way.

Meanwhile, *Titanic* was sinking lower and water began to flow over her bows. When the first boats had been lowered there had been order and calm. No one, including many of the crew, believed the ship would sink. Only those who had been party to the discussions in the wheelhouse were sure of *Titanic*'s fate. Those who had seen and heard about the steamer in the distance believed they would be saved, but as time went by and *Titanic* settled lower and lower into the water, they became less sure. Was this 'unsinkable' ship really going to sink? As more and more lifeboats left the ship, the passengers and remaining crew did not need a maths degree to see that there were hundreds more people left on the ship and definitely not enough lifeboats to go around. When, we may wonder, was the pivotal moment when everyone saw what hideous fate stood before them?

As Lightoller continued lowering boats on the port side, Murdoch was doing the same on the starboard deck. The weight this man carried on his shoulders must have been immense. He had been on duty on the bridge, and when she hit it had been his responsibility to navigate. He had been entrusted with the lives of over 2,200 people. He must have known his life was over and that he would not be leaving the ship. The least he could do as the end drew near was to get as many people into the boats as he could. Finding enough women to fill them was becoming a problem, but there must still be a lot more second- and third-class ladies; where were they? The first boats to have been lowered were filled well below their capacity. Tests in Belfast had showed that boats lowered with their full capacity of seventy men had no undue problems, yet some of the officers on *Titanic* believed that if they were to fill the boats from the davits the weight of the people would make them buckle in the middle, so many had been going out half full. Anyway, some of the boats would return soon from dropping off survivors at the steamer they had seen – wouldn't they?

The situation was becoming desperate, and now as many people as possible were being crammed in before the boats went down to the water. The mood of the steerage passengers flooding the boat deck was starting to get ugly. Groups of men, some foreigners, were starting to push and shove in an effort to get to the few remaining boats. Shots were being fired into the air and the officers and other members of the crew were having to drag men out of the boats by their arms, feet, or any part they could get a grip of. One man had been helping to fill the boats on the starboard side; a first-class passenger with striped pyjamas sticking out the bottom of his suit trousers, handing over many ladies into the waiting boats. But by now the man, Bruce Ismay, would be able to see the situation was looking grim, and he knew what the fate of the ship was going to be. He also knew that there were not nearly enough lifeboats. There was only one Engelhardt collapsible boat left on the starboard side. Ismay could see no further women on the deck around him. The collapsible Engelhardt C was filling up rapidly and a crowd of men was witnessed surging towards it. Two shots rang out and there were screams; passengers later reported to have seen men lying shot on the deck. Quartermaster Rowe watched as the pyjama-wearing passenger calmly climbed into the boat of his own accord. As collapsible C began to descend, the orders came over the side from Chief Officer Henry Wilde, 'All right, lower away.'

The band that had been playing earlier in the first-class smoking room had come out on deck to help calm everyone by playing ragtime tunes as the boats were being prepared to leave. Now, as it became clear there were no more boats and no more chance of being rescued, the music changed to more sombre melodies and hymns that would be remembered and immortalised by all that heard them in years to come.

Down in the depths of the ship the entire engineering and electrical team, with the help of many of the firemen, struggled to pump out the water and keep the lights and electricity working. But as the ship tilted higher and higher, a menacing creaking sound reverberated around the steel hull, followed by loud cracking sounds as the boilers and bulkheads started to rip away from their metal moorings. The huge leviathan prepared to tear herself in half as hundreds of tons of steel broke away and lurched towards the bow; crushing the men in an enormous metal tomb.

Robert had no coat or hat; he was bitterly cold and his lips were becoming frostbitten. Without a visible moon and a mile away from the ship, the dark closed in all around them like a black cloak, the candle in their lantern giving off only a pathetic glow. One woman in the boat was wailing and crying. Some of the ladies later said they thought she was calling for her son in French. It was Madame de Villiers; maybe she was calling for her lover Quigg. The night was beautiful. Stars filled the sky and the water was a black, silky millpond. The occupants of lifeboat 6 described *Titanic* as looking magnificent, with every one of her portholes lit up. Then as the passengers looked on, her stern started to rise out of the water slowly, higher and higher, and then she began her final descent. The occupants of lifeboat 6 looked on as *Titanic*'s lights flickered into darkness, transfixed as the great ship was lost to the sea.

Robert had not seen *Titanic* go down as he was facing in the other direction, and had been listening intently to the other boats calling to each other. As some didn't have lamps, this was the only way they could communicate. At least with Robert's lamp giving out some brightness, the other boats could navigate from him. It was very dark, however, and the lifeboats were scattered over a large area; Robert had no real idea how many there were or where they were. The light they had all been following seemed now to be getting further away. He didn't believe it was a steamer as he only saw one white masthead light, more likely a fishing vessel or a cod banker that had come up from Newfoundland. In years to come some would believe it had been a sailing ship called *Samson* out seal hunting illegally from Norway, and when they had seen the lights of the big ship, they had taken flight. Others believed it to be the *Californian*, a liner that would be blamed for not coming to their rescue when in fact it had been too far away and stuck in ice to have been of any help.

Titanic was gone and so was Robert's employment. White Star rules stated that if your ship should be wrecked your contract would cease with immediate effect and so would your pay. His family had been struggling hard for months with the strikes going on and now he was back where he started. But much worse, he had been at the wheel when the ship had struck the iceberg. He had got away with his life when hundreds of others, some of them his friends, would lose theirs. They all had their own private nightmare.

From far out on the dark sea another sound could be heard mixed in with the calls of the men from the lifeboats: the sound of hundreds of people screaming in the distance, crying as they floated helplessly among the debris that was all that was left of *Titanic*. From nearly a mile away the sound was like one, long continuous wail, no distinction between one voice and another. For the lifeboats that had left last and were nearer to the ship it must have been harrowing to witness. In lifeboat 4, Quartermaster Perkis was in charge. They were close enough to the ship to pick up eight people from the water. They had only been in the sea for a few minutes but the icy waters were a rapid killer and two of them died shortly after they were hauled on board. The passengers in his boat wrapped them up as best they could and rubbed their bodies hard to keep their circulation going. Only one other lifeboat from the sixteen on the water, No.14 commanded by Fifth Officer Lowe, was to go back for survivors that night, and he himself testified that he had not returned until the mayhem in the water had subsided. The passengers or the crew in the other boats had been too frightened of the massive suction the sinking liner would cause and had rowed away as fast as they could. In actuality, *Titanic* would create very little suction, but who was to know that? Those who were further away were terrified that if they went back to the people in the water they would be swamped and their boats would capsize, so they retreated to a safe distance to lay on their oars; the sounds of the dying would haunt them for the rest of their lives.

No one could ever forget listening to the wretched people in the water, wailing in distress. The screams were the stuff of night-mares and many survivors held awful memories and suffered symptoms of trauma from this sound alone. It was a memory Robert would never forget for as long as he lived, too. Although it continued only minutes, it was as if time stood still with only the blackness, the cold and the futility. The light they had been following had moved even further away and no other ship could be seen. They were hundreds of miles from land with no food, no compass and the temperature continued to fall – or so it seemed. If the weather turned or a storm hit them, they would be tossed into the sea to join the other poor victims. Robert was a man of the sea. He knew it was a wicked tormentor that claimed many lives, including his older brother Phillip who had drowned while out on a fishing trip years before. But it wasn't just his life on the line here; he had a boatload of frightened women he was trying to get to safety – wherever that might be. Should they row north or south? Without a compass they would end up rowing in circles. How long did they have left to float in this impenetrable blackness – hours, days? There must have been many unanswered questions.

The women began to insist that Robert go back to pick up those in the water; understandably fearful that their menfolk might be among them. Although Robert explained that with-out a compass and with no moon it would be impossible to find the way back, they insisted. Margaret Brown in her memoirs and newspaper interviews (and to anyone who would listen to her), gave the following account of what happened. In her contribu-tion to Archibald Gracie's book *Titanic, A Survivor's Story*, she described Robert as 'shivering like an aspen' and bursting out in a frightened voice the fate that awaited them, describing how she warned them the ship would draw everything around for miles around down with her suction and if they escaped that, the boil-ers would burst and rip up the bottom of the sea, tearing the icebergs asunder and completely submerging them. Apparently Robert had said that they were doomed either way. She went on to explain how Robert 'stood on his pinnacle trembling, with an attitude like someone preaching to the multitude, fanning the air with his hands and telling those in the boat that they would drift for days'. In Kirstin Iverson's book *Molly Brown, Unravelling the Myth*, she writes of how Helen Candee demanded, 'We must go back!' Mabel Martin adding, 'Yes, go back! Go back! We can fit a great many people in this boat,' to which Robert replied, 'No! It is our lives now, not theirs. Row damn you, our boat will immediately be swamped if we go back into all that confusion.' Another passenger by the name of Julia Cavendish then added, 'But there are a great many people in the water.' 'No!' Hichens shouted, 'We would go to our own deaths! They would only pull us down. Row! Row!' For the *New York Times* she stated:

> We stood him patiently and then after he told us we had no chance, told us many times and after he explained that we had no food, no water and no compass, I told him to be still or he would go overboard. Then he was quiet. I rowed because I would have frozen to death. I made them all row. It saved their lives.

It is not surprising that in later years Robert was known to often say to his family, 'She could have walked into any lifeboat, why oh why did she have to walk into mine?' In all the panic and heightened emotions of this night it is reasonable to accept that there were harsh words spoken and manners forgotten. Robert would later make a statement at the Inquiry as to what happened from his point of view.

Finally, Robert instructed his passengers to lay down their oars so that they could rest. Then out of the darkness came a shadow, which turned into another wooden lifeboat, and he could just see the number 16 on the side and a face, the face of the master at arms Joseph Bailey. The men shouted over to each other and Bailey came alongside. Robert and Fleet removed their lifejackets and slid them down between the two boats making fast to each other with a rope. This had been the first time in three hours that Robert had sat down and he was aching with the stiffness in his body. The women were exhausted and disheartened. Outer garments were shared for those who were shivering and whatever blankets could be spared were handed around. Mrs Candee offered up a half wet blanket to Robert and another lady draped it around his shoulders. Hélène Baxter had produced her small silver flask and offered it to Robert and he took it gratefully in shaking hands, sipping a spoonful, the liquor warming him for a few welcome minutes.

Gradually the light started to change. Grey began to seep through the black, and in the east a sorrowful dawn gradually broke revealing an incredible sight. One, two, three and more huge icebergs: mountains of ice 300ft high came into view. As the leaden sky turned to a dirty pink, more bergs became visible and waves could be heard splashing against their silvery sides. Other lifeboats came into view; appearing as dots on the horizon. It was now 4a.m. One of the ladies with a clipped British accent called and pointed and far in the distance a rocket exploded high up in the sky from the location they had rowed from, more than 2 miles away, 'A ship, a ship has come to save us.' Molly Brown was climbing all over the boat, giving orders: 'Sit down there, sit down!' Robert had had enough of this brash, loud Yank. 'I'll give the orders round here.' Then he called over to Bailey, 'Can you spare one of your men to help us?' On Bailey's confirmation a grimy fireman quickly climbed over the boats and sat down, reaching for an oar. He was never identified.

Robert only knew of Molly Brown from what he had seen of her in the lifeboat and that was quite enough. But she hadn't cranked up to full throttle yet; the best was still to come. The woman leaned over to the fireman and shouted at him to cut the rope free. Robert made to stop her; she stood to attention, and the two squared up to each other, spitting venom. Molly fumed, 'If you take one more step towards me, I'll throw you overboard.' Through some coaxing by the others Robert and Molly were persuaded to go back to their places, Bailey undid the ropes, and they were on their way. The ladies in the boat had been out on the Atlantic for four hours now. They were cold, extremely tired and terribly worried, not knowing whether their loved ones were alive or dead. They weren't ready for grief but they were ready for blame. They needed to vent their frustrations and Robert, with his sharp tongue and brusque manner – as well as being lower in rank than those brave, noble men on *Titanic* – would be the victim. He became the coward where the officers and the men left behind on the ship were the heroes. He hadn't gone back for survivors – but nor had the majority of other lifeboats for the same reasons as he. He wouldn't row, keeping to his position at the tiller, and so the more militant women felt they had plenty enough reasons to goad and taunt Robert.

In contrast, Molly hadn't left loved ones on *Titanic* and was a pragmatic and strong character to have with them. From this night she would become a heroine in their time of need, henceforth christened 'the unsinkable Molly Brown'. As for Major Peuchen, not only would he need to protect himself for being a man and getting into a lifeboat, but he was not going to let Robert forget how he had treated him earlier. From now on they rowed mainly in silence, intent on reaching their goal. As the other boats began to come together, the crew called over offering encouragement and seeing who was in the other boats; Robert was heard continually asking if anyone knew which officer had been on watch. Molly Brown encouraged the others to join her in singing some backwater tunes from her hometown. It raised the spirits of the women so Robert stood at his tiller and kept quiet, and they continued, with just over a mile to reach sanctuary.

7

RESCUE

Captain Rostron had turned in for a few hours' sleep when he received the distress call from *Titanic* at 12.35a.m., Monday 15 April. His ship, *Carpathia*, had left New York on Thursday and was on route via Liverpool and Gibraltar to Fiume in Austro-Hungary. The 13,000-ton steamer was carrying fifty first-class, fifty second and 560 steerage passengers, many of whom were German or Hungarian nationals returning home. As soon as the message came through, Rostron had ordered the ship to be turned round and headed directly for the location given to him by one of his officers, at latitude 41° 46' north, longitude 50° 14' west. The captain ordered all available power diverted to increase steam, and extra stokers were called on duty to fire up all boilers to get *Carpathia*'s maximum speed up. He knew they were heading for the ice region as it had been ice that had scuppered *Titanic*, and as standard procedure he put extra officers on the bridge and more lookouts in the bows.

Whilst steaming to the rescue, Rostron ordered everything to be made ready for whatever emergency situation they were heading towards. Doctors were summoned and all available medical supplies gathered. Tea, coffee and stronger stimulants, blankets and spare clothing were all arranged. Steerage berths would be cleared if necessary for survivors and the master at arms was called to supervise the current sleeping passengers' removal if necessary. At 2.30a.m. Rostron entered the ice region and for the next hour was passing bergs of every size, having to make hasty diversions and intricate changes of direction. They were powering at 19¼ knots, their full speed, with much risk to his own passengers and crew, but not a second could be wasted for time was critical in the freezing north Atlantic. When *Carpathia* arrived at the scene the gangway doors were opened with chair slings at the ready. Pilot ladders, nets overhanging the sides, boatswain chairs and canvas ash bags for children were all put in place. Rostron thought of everything, and having sent up a few rescue rockets at 4.10a.m., the first lifeboat was spotted and *Carpathia*'s engines were slowed and finally stopped.

Robert and his survivors had now been on the cold, black sea for seven hours. During that time, in below freezing temperatures, they had rowed to keep from succumbing to hypothermia; all of them suffering from shock and exhaustion and still in total disbelief that *Titanic* had sunk. In a few hours this desperate boatload of wrecked victims would learn that they were some of only 705 other survivors from a total of 2,228; that meant 1,523 passengers of the mail steamer SS *Titanic* on route to New York on her maiden voyage were missing, presumed dead.

At 8a.m. lifeboat 6 was the last to approach *Carpathia*. Robert had stood at the tiller for almost the entire journey, a half-sodden blanket draped around his shoulders. Looking up at the steamer, so very much smaller than *Titanic*, arms were outstretched by all the crew above and at the gangplanks to the side, welcoming the victims aboard with the utmost care. Babies and young children were hoisted up in the ash bags, and those not in pain or injured climbed up the ladders and nets or were strapped to chairs and pulled up. Some of the lifeboats had berthed by the gangplanks and their passengers walked wearily up into the hold. The entire procedure had taken four hours. As Robert's boat had been one of the first to leave *Titanic* and had rowed furthest away, it was now the last to reach the rescue ship. Having seen all those in his care to safety the exhausted quartermaster climbed up the ladder to be drawn into the waiting arms of the sympathetic crew above.

Looking down at the sea from the boat deck above, one solitary body could be seen, just one; a seaman floating on his side, his lifejacket keeping him bobbing on the choppy waves. The water splashed over his face, which bore no expression, just with the appearance of sleep. Cork and some wreckage was scattered about, but hardly any. Where were all the others and the rest of the wreckage? Had the currents carried everything and everyone away so soon? It would be five days later when a first-class passenger, Mrs Johanna Stunke, gave this vivid description of what she saw on the ship *Bremen*:

It was between four and five o'clock on Saturday when our ship sighted off the bow to the starboard, an iceberg. We had been told by some of the officers that the *Bremen* was going to pass within a few miles of the position given by the *Titanic* when she sank, so when the cry went up that ice was sighted we all rushed to the starboard rail. It was a beautiful afternoon and the sun glistening on the big iceberg was a wonderful picture, but as we drew nearer and could make out small dots floating around in the sea a feeling of awe and sadness crept over every one, and the ship proceeded in absolute silence. We passed within one hundred feet of the southern most drift of the wreckage, and looking down over the rail we distinctly saw a number of bodies so clearly that we could make out what they were wearing and whether they were men or women. We saw one woman in her nightdress with her baby clasped closely to her breast. Several of the women passengers screamed and left the rail in a fainting condition. There was another woman, fully dressed, with her arms tight around the body of a shaggy dog that looked like a St. Bernard. [There had indeed been a St Bernard on board *Titanic* owned by a lady.] The bodies of three men in a group; all clinging to one steamer chair, floated close by and just beyond them were a dozen bodies of men, all in life-preservers, clinging together as though in the last desperate struggle for life.[25]

There would be similarly harrowing accounts in the newspapers as the days progressed.

On *Carpathia* Robert could see icebergs surrounding them at every compass point. The day had turned out grey and insipid, and the scene that would have presented itself to Robert was no less heartrending. One woman knelt on the deck beating her chest, rocking back and forth with great tears pouring down her face. A *Carpathia* steward walked by clutching the hands of two boys, not more than four years old, with no idea what was happening to them or where their mother and father might be. Wives and daughters were going in one door and out another, pacing the ship, wanting to see the faces of their beloved husbands or fathers – but at each turn there was only disappointment and, thoroughly beaten, they would sink into chairs and bow their heads. Robert went into the dining room and found a small group of crew he knew in the corner. He joined them and as they were discussing the events of the previous night, Molly Brown and some of the other women from the lifeboat had gathered nearby, listening and watching him intently.[26] They were not going to forgive him for not returning to the ship. Robert would not know now, but these women were all to make statements to journalists and writers that would seal a reputation for him that went a long way towards ruining his life. He moved away from his group and left the room.

In the Inquiry that was to follow, Charles Lightoller would testify to having spoken to the lookouts, whilst on the *Carpathia*, about what they had seen. As the most senior surviving officer, one might ask, which other crew members did he speak to in those first hours? Bruce Ismay was meanwhile being administered opiates in the surgeon's cabin, suffering from shock. *Carpathia* passengers did not take long to get out their notebooks and start grilling the survivors, amongst them Howard Chapin, Mr and Mrs Charles Hutchinson and Miss May Birkhead.[27] It would have been imperative for the crew to have their stories straight before any uncompromising discussions took place. The most crucial witnesses Lightoller would have to speak to would be Fleet, Lee and Robert Hichens. It would seem that, soon into the voyage, Robert would already have had his sanitised party line neatly and succinctly executed.[28] He would then not waiver from his account, which would be the one he would stand up and testify to in seven days' time in front of the Senate Committee in Washington. Lightoller would also need to talk to the officers Pitman, Boxhall and Lowe and the other key witnesses, quartermasters Rowe and Olliver. The crew needed to have their stories 'correct', knowing that there would be an inquiry in England. They were not to know that there would be an inquiry in New York at this time, but nothing should be overlooked. By the time the important witnesses had arrived in New York, they had been 'drilled' in the company rules. In the IMM's *Ships Rulebook and Uniform Regulations* it was laid down that 'if it can be avoided, no declaration should be made before a Receiver of Wreck until instructions have been obtained'; instructions in this case, by the White Star Line.

After the four hours it had taken to get everyone on board, Rostron organised a short service for all with prayers for the living and the departed. *Carpathia* had cruised around for a while but no other bodies were found. The *Californian*, which had previously been stuck in the ice, had also arrived on the scene and when the two captains had exchanged words, Rostron bade farewell and turned his ship around to make the four-day journey back to New York. On Monday 15 April, Captain Rostron sent a message concerning the sinking, rescue and survivors. The following messages were also written by Bruce Ismay: 'Deeply regret to advise, Titanic sunk this morning 15th after collision with iceberg, resulting serious loss of life, particulars later.' Rostron endorsed the letter but it went unsent until 9a.m., Wednesday 17th. Word had it that the wireless operator had held it back for some reason. On the 17th Ismay sent a number of messages which were intercepted by Naval offices on their way to Phillip Franklin, vice president at IMM offices:

Most desirable *Titanic* crew aboard '*Carpathia*' should be returned home earliest possible. Suggest you hold '*Cedric*', sailing her Friday unless you see any reason on contrary. Propose returning on her myself. Please send outfits of clothes including shoes for me to '*Cedric*'. Have nothing of my own, please reply. YAMSI. [Ismay's private code.]

Very important you should hold '*Cedric*' daylight Friday for *Titanic* crew, answer.

Think most unwise to keep *Titanic* crew until Saturday. Strongly urge detaining '*Cedric*', sailing her midnight if desirable.

The crew and passengers of *Carpathia* could not do enough for the unfortunate *Titanic* victims. All the survivors could do now was to accept the care and compassion offered to them and get through the next four days of the return journey to New York; the weather of the smooth early journey on *Titanic* had now turned stormy and unpleasant.

8

⇥ NEW YORK ⇤

As 9.30p.m. approached on Thursday evening, *Carpathia* sailed towards pier 54 and great torrents of rain fell mixed with loud rumbles of thunder and forks of white lightning. Waiting for the ship were 40,000 onlookers, friends and relatives of the passengers. When an early wireless message had been sent telling of *Titanic* being towed to Halifax in England, a number of relatives had immediately taken the train there, only for them to have to return to New York.[29] The harbour was crowded with small craft and filled with reporters shouting and flashing their cameras, eager to get the first pictures and news stories for their front pages. The *New York Times* was there, up front with many of their best and most cunning reporters. There were rumours too that the Marconi company had arranged a deal with *The New York Times*; they had certainly been the first newspaper to confirm the *Titanic's* sinking, and there was no way they were going to miss another opportunity here at the pier.

Many of *Titanic's* steerage passengers stayed on *Carpathia* while it was decided what could be done for them. Immigration authorities came on board to check their papers while *Carpathia* passengers disembarked; their Mediterranean journey to Hungary would be postponed for now. The silent sobbing of many of the onlookers turned to near hysteria as, one by one, the second and then the first-class passengers made their way slowly down the gangplank. There were tears of joy as relatives were reunited, mixed with wails of despair as others learned the fate of their loved ones. Some fainted as the crowds pushed nearer and nearer to get a first glimpse of their family members. Reportedly, one man came lunging to the front, looking completely mad with foam spitting out the corners of his mouth, crying out 'my sister, my sister, is she alive?', before the authorities realised he was just another hack. 'I'll pay two hundred dollars!' he shouted, begging for a story from one of the survivors before he was promptly despatched by a burly policeman.

One small, officious-looking group of men moved quickly through the crowd brandishing documents and signatures, and they were immediately let on to the *Carpathia*. Senator William Alden Smith headed the group and there was one man he needed to see before any other: Bruce Ismay. An officer led the group through to the centre of the ship to the surgeon's quarters and Smith knocked on Ismay's door, where a sign hung which read 'please do not knock'. A tall, rather good-looking man with a dark handlebar moustache appeared. Smith introduced himself and Ismay swung the door open to receive his visitor. The senator would be in conference with him for the next half an hour.

Senator Smith was a highly successful Republican lawyer from Michigan in his late fifties. Two days after the sinking he had taken the floor of the Senate to propose a special investigation under the auspices of the Senate Commerce Committee. His resolution, unanimously approved, authorised a panel to investigate the causes leading to the wreck of the White Star Line's *Titanic*. The panel would be given authority to summon witnesses, administer oaths and take the necessary testimonies. Two days before, Smith had heard about the messages that had been picked up by the Naval offices from Bruce Ismay. The suggestion was that the White Star boss had planned to spirit himself and his crew back to England without setting foot on US soil. Smith wanted to make sure no one culpable in the disaster escaped American jurisdiction. It would turn out that as the British citizens were on US soil, and that ultimately the ship belonged to an American trust, the committee had full jurisdiction to hold the men until such a time as the testimonies had been heard – and until Smith was satisfied he had all the facts pertaining to the disaster.

The senator had gone to the White House and received President William Howard Taft's authorisation to set about his investigations. Taft was a very unhappy man: when he had heard about the disaster he had immediately sent scouts out by sea to get first-hand news, to find out what had happened, and to get news about his good friend and aide Archibald Butt. The message had apparently been blocked by *Carpathia's* wireless room, and this had angered the president greatly. Smith, although not a nautical man, was a popular and successful lawyer. He was an expert interrogator and had an almost photographic memory, as well as being able to absorb and mentally process large amounts of information. He could extract valuable details from even the most unwilling of witnesses. He wanted to know why *Titanic* had foundered with the loss of over 1,500 lives. His mission would be to question such things as the increased speed of the vessel on the night of the wreck, when it had previously received at least four warnings of bergs and field ice by other ships during the day of the tragedy, some of which were stopped in the ice. Why were the many indications of ice that night apparently ignored? His committee would challenge those responsible to give him answers as to whether adequate safety inspections had been carried out, and he would grill the Board of Trade who had authorised the number of lifeboats on board – causing hundreds to be left behind on the stricken ship. He would leave no stone unturned in his quest to discover why this catastrophe had occurred and would take important and historical steps to ensure nothing like this could ever happen in the future. [30]

When the meeting with Ismay had ended, Smith produced a list of the surviving officers and twenty-eight of the crew he believed could help him with his inquiries. The crew that needed to be questioned would be held on another White Star Line ship, *Celtic*, and the senator would issue subpoenas for them to appear before the committee, starting with Ismay, the following morning. The rest of the crew would be held on the Red Star Line *Lapland* until their return to England on Saturday. However, included on the *Lapland* crew list were two key witnesses that had been overlooked by the senator, or more likely deliberately held back, for reasons that would become apparent later. They were Lookout Reginald Lee and Quartermaster Robert Hichens. As the chosen witnesses were escorted off *Carpathia*, the rest of the crew were mustered on deck and reportedly seen being marched down the pier under the watchful protection of security officers and taken to the *Lapland*. Many of the crew had asked to be allowed to go ashore, but were refused and ordered back in line.

Journalists watched as Frederick Fleet and the rest of the sub-poenaed crew were taken, under guard, by private detectives to the *Celtic*. Here the journalists were told that the crew were under strict instructions, and that they would be dismissed from the White Star Line's service for good if it was ascertained that any of them had disobeyed the instructions against talking. One reporter from the *New York Times*, unaware of the restrictions and the close guard in place, wanted to get to Frederick Fleet to hear his story about events on the night of the tragedy. Somehow he managed to get past the guards and a sailor led him down two decks into the crew's mess room. Here the men were in the middle of their meal of corned beef and mashed potato, washed down with coffee. The reporter sat at the end of the table amongst six of the crew and, when he asked what had occurred up in the crow's nest, Fleet reportedly said:

> Not a word, except when I get my hands on that guy what gave out the story about me – him that was running the wheel – why, when I get my hands on him, he'll be lucky to know if his name's Hichens or Hawkins. He said he saw me in the crow's nest. Now, there was a cabin in between and he saw nothing of me at all and what's more, he ain't one of us.

Fleet then went on to say that Hichens the quartermaster was making his first trip and hadn't been 'drilled' in the sailor's way of 'sitting tight and waitin' for the boss's word'. He went on to add that as for himself, he had been 'drilled' and so when Mr Ismay said not to talk, as far as he was concerned, there was 'nothing to be said'. Even though Fleet had been told to keep his mouth shut, he was having a little difficulty in remembering the 'drill'. What he didn't mention was that he was being offered a pension for life by his employers the White Star Line on condition that he kept silent at the forthcoming inquiry about the early iceberg warn-ings.[31] After this the discussions turned to how much some of the sailors would receive for giving out their stories and how much they would get from the relief funds being raised in New York and England. Fleet felt confident that their boss, Bruce Ismay, would look after them and he had already intimated that wages would be paid up to the time of getting home again.

They were a sorry lot who spent their first night on the *Lapland*. In New York the city had opened its arms to the stricken passengers and offers of money, food and clothing were in great supply. In contrast, Robert and the stokers, seamen and stewards were still in the same clothes and were penniless. Many had lost friends or family who had worked with them on *Titanic*, and all had lost their jobs when the ship sank. On Saturday morning, the day of their departure back to England, they had been invited to a memorial service at the American Seamen's Friend Society at 507 West Street. Before the service the Revd Dr George McPherson Hunter, who would be conducting the proceedings, sent the men over to the Women's Relief Committee at the Metropolitan Building to receive new clothes and money. The stewardesses had already been visited at the *Lapland* with help, and although the charity had been gratefully accepted by the crew, they felt bitter that the White Star Line had given them nothing and no financial remuneration at all. A reporter from the *New York Times* followed the story:

Two of Titanic's seamen both of whom were active in the work of saving lives after the ship hit the iceberg appeared yesterday at the office of the Women's Relief Committee in the Metropolitan Building and asked for help. One was R R Lee, one of the two lookouts in the crow's nest of the steamship when she hit the iceberg and the other was Robert Hichens, the quartermaster. Both said they were through with the sea. Lee says that when he gets back to England he is going to stay on dry land and become a life insurance agent. The Rev McPherson Hunter of the American Seamen's Friend Institute had sent the two sailors to the Committee. Rev Hunter said the two men had done good work and needed help. They got it.

Lee told the members of the Committee who asked him questions that he and the members of the crew weren't drunk when the accident occurred. He said he had read it in the papers and he didn't want anyone to think that it was true. He had been in the Royal Navy, he said and when the ship struck, both he and his partner in the crow's nest, Frederick Fleet who testified yesterday before the Senate Committee in Washington, were wide awake and on watch. He told the Committee that he had a wife but he hadn't seen her for nine years.[32] He did not want much from the Committee, just a few shillings he said. The White Star Line wouldn't pay him his wages until he got back to England and he wanted a little spending money in the meantime.

Hichens told the Committee that he had a wife and two children in England and he was afraid they were in trouble and they needed money. Hichens wouldn't talk about the disaster; he kept telling the Committee about his family in England. So they gave him some money but instead of taking it for himself, he went downstairs straight away and bought a money order with the whole sum and sent it off to England. He will get some more today.

In another article from *The New York Times* it was reported that 100 crew from the *Lapland* stood in the little assembly hall at the Seamen's Friend Institute, the Revd Hunter lifted his hands in prayer: 'To the one who had brought them out of the peril of the great deep …' After reciting the Lord's Prayer many of the congregation could hardly hold back their tears and there was much coughing and blowing into handkerchiefs. When Josephine Upham took her place many of the crowd stood up and applauded her; a matron and missionary, she had known many of these crew from previous visits to New York. As the opening strains of *Nearer My God to Thee* flowed through the room, for a moment the terrible experiences that had affected them were forgotten, and Robert joined the others to sing their hymns of the sea at the top of their voices. *Rock of Ages* was followed by *For Those in Peril on the Sea*. When the service finally ended the hosts and their guests joined for coffee and sandwiches and spent some time recounting their stories to those who offered sympathy and friendship.

Back on the *Lapland* later that day, the crew prepared for the long trip back to England. The ship would sail into Plymouth on 28 April and then Robert would catch the train to Southampton. Leaving the dock, the *Lapland* slowly proceeded out of New York Harbour and up the Hudson River. As the crew gazed out at the grey sea they could see a tug following in their wake. They waited for it to pass but instead the *Lapland*'s engines slowed and finally stopped and three men came on board. They were officials, headed by a man called Joe Bayliss, who had been sent from the Senate Department, and they were after five of the crew which included Reginald Lee and one in particular – Robert Hichens. The five were being taken back to New York; their services were required and it had become imperative these men were subpoenaed to appear before the Senate Committee in three days' time.

9

NEW YORK HEARINGS

While Robert had been incarcerated on the *Lapland*, the Inquiry
had begun at 10a.m. on Friday 19 April, the morning after
Carpathia had brought back the survivors. In New York's Waldorf
Astoria, the East Room would be the setting for the first day of
the Inquiry. In the centre of the lavish surroundings was a large
conference table and in all corners of the room were members of
the press and public; there was standing room only. In a high-back
chair sat Bruce Ismay, managing director of White Star Line and
chairman of International Mercantile Marine. He was accompanied by the president of IMM, Phillip Franklin, two lawyers and
two bodyguards. It had been reported that Ismay had started to
receive death threats as much of the blame, the public felt, rested
on the shoulders of the man who ultimately owned the ship and
who should have gone down with her as had Captain Smith.
From an almost complete breakdown on the *Carpathia*, Ismay
now appeared immaculately dressed in a tailored suit. His dark
complexion and well-groomed handlebar moustache gave him
the air of English nobility. Seated next to Ismay was senior surviving second officer, Charles Herbert Lightoller, who the press
described as being a square-jawed powerfully built man, perfectly
at ease in front of the committee.

Senator Smith opened the meeting by making the resolu-
tions he had discussed and had agreement with from President
Taft. He would take testimonies from members of the crew;
passengers; the ship's designers, builders and owners; wireless

operators; hydrographical organisations and all who could give him the answers he needed. He was aware that members of the senior crew – Chief Officer Wilde, First Officer Murdoch, Sixth Officer Moody and of course, Captain Smith – had perished, so it would be down to the remaining officers to explain the events of Sunday night. First, he wanted to speak to the owner of *Titanic*.

Bruce Ismay was therefore the first to take the stand. Senator Smith grilled Ismay on the wholly inadequate number of life-boats, which saved but a third of the passengers and crew aboard the ship. Ismay answered that the numbers were in line with Board of Trade regulations, and in fact there were four more than were required by law. He vehemently denied that he had wanted to push *Titanic* to go faster even though two key witnesses would testify that they had heard him say just that. To the question of his departure in a lifeboat, Ismay responded that he had helped many women and children into the boats and only when no more were left on deck did he take his place on collapsible boat C, which was the second-to-last to leave on the starboard side before the ship went down. He said he had briefly visited the bridge after the impact and was told the situation was serious and that she was badly damaged. He had been travelling to New York as a passen-ger, purely to see how *Titanic* performed on her first voyage and to see what improvements could be made. For now, the senator had finished with Ismay, but that would not be the end; he was not going to let him off that easily.

As the afternoon progressed it was the second officer, Charles Lightoller, who came into Smith's sights. This man would play a major role in both the US and British Inquiries as the senior sur-viving officer. Larger than life, his background read like a novel. Born in 1874, Charles Lightoller was to lose his mother just months after his birth and he and his sisters were brought up by their father. The strain of rearing the children appeared too great for him though, and he abandoned his family and went to New Zealand, instead leaving them to be raised by an aunt and uncle who felt very burdened by the responsibility and didn't let the children forget it. At thirteen, Lightoller left home for a life at sea, during the time when sail was still the method of propulsion. He encountered violent storms, cyclones and coal fires bringing him close to death on many occasions. From sail, Lightoller turned to steam ships, and while in port in Africa contracted malaria, which nearly killed him. Taking a break from the sea he went on to pan for gold in the rush of the 1890s in Canada, and then became a cowboy for a stretch before working his way back to England. At twenty-five Lightoller returned to the sea and in 1900 joined the White Star Line.[33]

While docked in Australia he met Sylvia Hawley-Wilson, who before long he would marry. Sylvia had been born with a foot deformity and spent her young life in leg irons and having to use sticks. An attempt at surgery was unsuccessful but she was strong in her faith and walked unaided with a pronounced limp, uncomplaining and resolute. It was on a visit to New York that Lightoller would discover a new religion that would change his and Sylvia's life: Mary Eddy Baker had been injured as a child and was very sickly throughout her young life and one day, after reading a passage in her bible, she came to believe that God had spoken to her. Over the years she subsequently created her own interpretation of the bible's message, and in 1876 wrote a Christian Science textbook called *Science, Health with Key to Scriptures*. Baker's branch of Christian Scientists believed that God and all he created was spiritual and not material: sickness, death, sin and evil and all things material – including the human body – do not exist. Matter and death are mortal illusions and the 'spirit' is the key. Doctors, medicine and surgery must be avoided, as prayer alone is the healer. In times of adversity, danger or illness the human spirit will be protected by God's goodness and be made indestructible, eternal and beyond sin. It was their devotion to this 'modern' religion that gave support to Sylvia to help her overcome her disability, and strength for Lightoller when he was soon to come face to face with death once more, and be questioned on his infallible character.

Even though it was for one trip only, demotion to second officer had been tough for Lightoller as he had already served as first officer on both the *Majestic* and *Oceanic* White Star liners, and his dream had been to one day command his own ship. But now it looked as though everything he had worked for was hanging in the balance. Not only would he have to protect himself and his remaining senior crew, he would need at all costs to protect his employers who held the key to his future success. Throughout the entire hearings Lightoller would be asked more questions than any other witness, all of which he answered in both a self-reliant and expertly evasive manner. His ability to blind Senator Smith with his nautical experience gave him the upper hand and he steadfastly defended the White Star Line, liberally applying the whitewash brush.[34] He explained the sea trials that had been made in Belfast and all the safety inspections that had been carried out in Southampton where *Titanic* was given a clean bill of health. Having described the smooth run for the first four days he was then to tell of his movements on the day of the disaster.

Lightoller had come on watch at 6p.m. on the evening of Sunday 14 April. At around 9p.m., the captain had arrived on the bridge and the two men talked about the calm and clear conditions of the evening. Lightoller had explained to the captain that he estimated they would be coming up to the ice region at about 11p.m., and they discussed how they would recognise ice if they should come across it, freshening up their minds for the hours ahead. They spoke for about twenty minutes and just before departing the captain told Lightoller that if there was any change in the conditions, and that if it was in the slightest degree hazy, there should be no doubt they would need to go very slowly. Importantly, at 9.30p.m. Lightoller had instructed Sixth Officer Moody to call up to the lookouts to warn them of small ice and growlers and to pass the word on; but there was no mention at this time of changes in condition or haze. Lightoller told the senator he had not seen any ice warnings that evening and believed the speed they were going was safe. At 10p.m. Murdoch had come to take over the watch and he and Lightoller had again discussed the clear weather conditions and the long distance for which they could see. He had passed on all the information about ice warnings and the captain's instructions, and then had left the bridge to conduct his usual tour around the ship before retiring. It looked as though Lightoller had done everything by the book and the conversation he said had taken place with the captain was very detailed (if indeed it took place at all; there were no witnesses to hear it and it rather appeared that by diverting blame away from himself he had placed it at the feet of the next officer on watch, First Officer William Murdoch).

Lightoller said he had been drifting off to sleep when he felt the impact. It was slight but, feeling the engines had stopped, he had left his cabin in his pyjamas two or three minutes later. Going on deck he had walked a few paces until he saw the first

officer on the corner of the outer bridge on the port side, looking out to sea. He then went back through his quarters and out
to the other side, and saw the captain in the same position on
the starboard side, also looking out to sea. The ship, he noticed,
had slowed down and was moving through the water at about
6 knots. He was returning to his cabin when he met Third Officer
Pitman, who had come out from his cabin, and they had a brief
chat about how they thought they had hit something, but being
cold and not thinking anything was seriously amiss they had both
returned to their berths. Lightoller went on to say that he had
been in his cabin for about ten minutes when Fourth Officer
Boxhall had come to tell him they had hit an iceberg and were
taking water. Lightoller had then gone to supervise the lowering
of the lifeboats.

During his testimony he explained that there was no panic,
everything had been calm and there had been no prevention of
steerage passengers getting to safety. He instructed the lifeboats
to head for a ship they thought was a steamer, and then he went
into some detail about how the ship had 'left him' and when he
was in the water he was sucked against the grate of a funnel. He
rescued himself by clambering onto an upturned lifeboat, which
eventually thirty other men joined. Another lifeboat came alongside them and they climbed aboard, then they were rescued by
Carpathia. For now, Lightoller was allowed to go but he would be
called back in four days' time for further questioning.

In the next few days the hearings moved to a larger room to
accommodate the ever-growing crowd of journalists and specta-
tors. Senator Smith and the other committee members continued
to question witnesses from the head of Marconi wireless and two
of their operators, and a first-class steward (who would tell the
tragic tale of the Straus couple who would not be parted and
who had stayed on the doomed liner to the end).

On day three Boxhall, the fourth officer, took the stand. He
was very nervous and had to be encouraged to speak up as he
sat wringing his hands. He was not a well man from his experience and the senator was aware he probably would not have long
to question him. Boxhall reported that he had come on duty at
8p.m. for his four-hour shift and had spent most of the evening
in the chart room. He had spoken to Lightoller during his watch
but he made no mention of seeing Murdoch at all through the

evening. He had met with the captain after 9p.m. to discuss the positions he had worked out, but could not be definite about seeing him again until after the collision. Boxhall then explained that he had been coming out of the officers' quarters and was just passing the captain's room on the starboard side when he heard three bells, and a moment later the grinding sound. He thought so little of it he didn't stop or adjust his pace. (He was in a prime position to have seen the iceberg passing by but he did not mention this.) He was approaching the bridge and heard the order 'Hard-a-starboard'. As he walked through the wheelhouse to the pilot room he saw Moody, Murdoch and the captain. Boxhall then said he heard Murdoch say, 'I put her "Hard-a-starboard" and ran her engines full astern but we were too close and we hit'.

If the ship had gone from 'full speed ahead' to 'full astern' in that short space of time there would have been an almighty vibration throughout the vessel that would have had passengers flying from their beds. Boxhall's testimony made no record of this effect, however. He instead recounted that Murdoch had gone on to say, 'I intended to port around it.' He then said Murdoch pushed the switch to close the watertight doors. The next thing they all did was to walk to the far corner of the open bridge to see the iceberg. Boxhall fancied he could see a very, very low-lying dark growler but he could not swear by it. The captain then ordered him below to see if there was any damage. Boxhall went down to steerage but saw none and returned to tell the captain. He was sent back down to tell the carpenter to sound the ship. Boxhall met the carpenter who said they were taking in water and Boxhall told him to go tell the captain. Then he met a mail clerk who said there was also water in the post room so Boxhall sent him to the captain too. He went down to see for himself and saw the clerks attempting to save the mailbags from the gushing flow. On returning to the captain once more, he was then ordered to go and see to the boats and that is what he did. There was no mention, contrary to Lightoller's testimony, of going to Lightoller's cabin.

After taking some of the lifeboat covers off, he'd gone back to the chart room to work out their position and then had gone down to the wireless room to give it to Bride and Phillips, with the instruction to call for help. Back at the bridge he was told to fire off rockets and use the Morse code equipment on deck to communicate with a ship they could see about 5 miles off the port bow. Boxhall's lifeboat had been the last-but-one to leave on the port side, and would be the first to reach the *Carpathia* in the morning. After this statement, Smith excused Boxhall.

Quartermaster Rowe, when he was questioned, explained how he had felt the grinding all the way back at the poop deck where he was stationed, and that he saw the berg which he thought looked like the sails of a windjammer going by in the dark. He had telephoned the fore bridge and been instructed to bring and then set off rockets with the fourth officer, he then went to command collapsible lifeboat C.

On Friday evening Ismay asked permission to leave on the *Lapland* and return to England the next day with the rest of the crew who were not going to be questioned, but the senator refused his request. Smith felt he owed it to the American public to keep him on US soil until every effort had been made to uncover the truth. He believed that the White Star Line and the senior surviving officer, Lightoller, were at best giving the most sanitised course of events, and at worst were concealing vital information which could prove negligence and culpability. If there was a case for negligence then the American survivors would be able to sue for vast sums of money from IMM, and that would put them into irreversible financial trouble. The British consul and IMM officials were up in arms at the detention of British subjects, and if the subjects stayed in the state of New York the consul might have been able to win the right to send the witnesses home. As such, Senator Smith made the decision to move the Inquiry to the capital, Washington, where there was a different jurisdiction that could keep them in the country, and made plans to do so the very next day. On Saturday morning he learned that a further five crucial witnesses had already set sail on the *Lapland* to return to England. He sent out his sheriff, Joe Bayliss, on a pilot boat to track them down and bring them back.

10

⊶ MOVE TO WASHINGTON ⊶

Robert must have been devastated not to be going home and would be worried sick about his family in James Street. The landlord would not wait too long for unpaid rent money, that was for sure. Once again the crew had a bad time of it in New York. Interviews with journalists told how they had asked representatives of IMM for some advance money on their wages as they were destitute, but were told that they would get none until they returned to England. They weren't even allowed to phone their anxious relatives at home and were told it would be too great an expense. They were taken to the *Celtic* with the other twenty-nine crew members who had been subpoenaed, but they would not be there for long as a train ride to Washington was to follow that afternoon. When they arrived at the nation's capital they were kept under guard by Senator Smith's secretary Bill McKinstry at the Continental Hotel. In Wynn Craig's book *Titanic, End of a Dream*, he describes how Lightoller believed he and the other three officers should not have to share a hotel with the lower-ranking crew. He wanted them to go to the same hotel as Ismay and Franklin, the expensive New Willard. Willard's management refused the request because they were not happy at the prospect of having rowdy crewmen upsetting their elegant clientele. Lightoller attempted to insist again and McKinstry exploded: 'My God, your Captain now sleeps with his crew, under the waves.' Lightoller requested that if they had to remain in the same hotel as the lower-ranking crew, then they should be on a separate floor and have their own dining area. This was agreed, however the next day the whole crew were moved to another hotel with individual rooms, the National.

The following morning the Inquiry began again in the new wing of the Senate Office building. Smith had become terribly frustrated for Ismay had, for the third time, pleaded with the senator to allow him to return home, saying he would put any amount of company representatives at his disposal. Once again the request was refused. Before the day started in earnest, Senator Smith stood and gave out an important notice:

> I desire to make an announcement ... We are not at all concerned about the convenience of visitors upon the Inquiry. We are concerned primarily in obtaining the truth and I desire each person here to understand that they are here solely by the courtesy of the Committee, that the Inquiry is not for their entertainment and that any expressions of any kind or character will not be permitted. (US Titanic Inquiry Project)

On day four, Third Officer Herbert Pitman took the stand. His watch had been from 6–8p.m. Pitman stated that during the evening he had seen Captain Smith once just before 7p.m. and also Lightoller, but had not spoken to him as he was in the chart room working out stellar observations. After further questioning he admitted that he had in fact spoken to Lightoller because they took a set of sights together between 7.30–7.40p.m. He also mentioned they'd had a conversation with some of the other men about the fact that they would be heading towards the ice region during Murdoch's watch; when pushed on this conversation, Pitman replied: 'Oh, I cannot remember now sir, when it occurred and I have now not the slightest idea who was there.'

Pitman said that he was in his bunk drifting off to sleep when he felt the impact, which he described as being like a chain running over the windlass. Thinking they were coming into anchor he had left his room in his nightclothes and had gone out to find out what was happening. Seeing nothing out of order, he returned to his berth and sat down to light his pipe. (There was no mention of a meeting with Lightoller on deck, again in contrast to Lightoller's earlier statement.) After a short while he thought he might get dressed as it was approaching his watch, and that was when Boxhall had come to tell him they had hit ice. (Again there is a contradiction here, as Boxhall made no mention of going to Pitman's cabin at the US hearing, but he did at the British hearing. In his testimony in Britain Boxhall only mentions going to Lightoller and Pitman's cabins. Surely the most important officer he should have woken would be Captain Smith's second in command, Chief Officer Wilde. There is no mention of Boxhall saying he went to his cabin, or to Officer Lowe's.) He went on to explain that he had gone down to the well deck and seen some ice there and had then gone up to the boat deck to await instructions from the other senior officers.

The remaining officer to take the stand on day five was Fifth Officer Harold Lowe. Lowe had been at sea most of his life and was very experienced in both sail and steam. He was also cocky, handsome and very popular with the ladies. His shift had also been between 6–8p.m. and he had been working out a slip table, which gave the position of the ship. When he had finished he had placed it on the captain's chart room desk before, allegedly, retiring to his berth. It was at this point that Senator Smith asked Lowe an interesting question, and the following conversation ensued:

S: Are you a temperate man?

L: I am sir. I never touched it in my life. I am an abstainer.

S: I am very glad to have you say that.

L: I say it sir, without fear of contradiction.

S: I am not contradicting you and I congratulate you upon it but so many stories have been circulated; one has just been passed up to me now from a very reputable man who says it was reported that you were drinking that night.

L: Me sir?

S: That is why I am asking the question.

L: No sir. This [he indicated to his glass of water], is the strongest drink I ever take.

Smith left it at that. He had previously posed the same simple question about temperance to Boxhall, who of course denied he'd had anything to drink as well.

Lowe told the senator that he had gone to bed between 8–8.30p.m. and was awakened when he heard voices, which he thought was strange. The impact hadn't woken him and he explained that as the crew had little sleep on a voyage, when they did sleep, it was the sleep of the dead. (It seems strange that the thunderous blowing off of steam directly outside his cabin had not woken him.) Lowe went on to testify that when he looked out of his cabin he saw lots of people on deck in lifejackets, so he jumped up, got dressed, grabbed his revolver and went outside where he felt as though the ship was tipping forward to a degree and he, like the other officers, had gone to assist with the lifeboats. Harold Lowe had been the only commander of a lifeboat to go back for survivors and, although picking four from the water, only two had survived. Lowe had also been rather 'trigger happy' but hadn't been seen shooting anyone.

Senator Smith excused Lowe. He had now questioned all of the officers and wanted to turn his attention to the lower-ranking crew members, starting with one of the lookouts who had been there when the iceberg was sighted. Frederick Fleet thus took the stand. The press were quick to notice how shabbily he was dressed in charity clothes from one of the missions in New York; his shoes were broken and the man looked very nervous in front of a packed audience. Journalists found him difficult to understand as, originally from Liverpool, Fleet had a strong accent, and in his anxious state he found it hard to communicate what he wanted to say. He stood twisting his cap in his hands. The twenty-four-year-old had been with the White Star Line for four years, making him a company man, and he had been 'drilled' at length by representatives of the company before his testimony and, more importantly, what not to say. He began by describing how clear the night had been with no moon, thousands of stars and the sea as calm as a millpond. Senator Smith asked:

> S: I want to get on the record the place you were stationed in the performance of your duty.
> F: I was on the lookout.
> S: In the crow's nest?
> F: Yes.
> S: Can you tell me how high above the boat deck that is?
> F: I have no idea.
> S: Can you tell me how high above the crow's nest the masthead is?
> F: No sir.

S: Do you know how far you were above the bridge?
F: I am no hand at guessing.
S: I do not want you to guess but if you know I would like to have you tell me.
F: I have no idea.

At this point Senator Fletcher took over the questioning:

SF: You hardly mean that. You have some idea?
F: No, I do not.
SF: You know whether it was a thousand feet or one hundred?

The questions progressed slowly, and Fleet gave nothing away. Senator Smith had been told in an earlier testimony from Captain Rostron of the *Carpathia* about the extra lookouts that had been stationed on his ship as they came to the ice region, and he wanted to find out if *Titanic* officers had ordered extra lookouts too:

S: Can you tell me who was on the most forward part of the *Titanic* Sunday night when you took your position in the crow's nest?
F: There was nobody.
S: Nobody?
F: No sir.

Smith turned to what had happened during the sighting of the iceberg:

S: Tell me what you did.
F: Well, I reported an iceberg right ahead, a black mass.
S: When did you report it?
F: I could not tell you the time.
S: At about what time?
F: Just after seven bells [11.30p.m.].
S: How long before the collision or accident did you report ice ahead?
F: I have no idea.
S: About how long?
F: I could not say the rate she was going.

> S: How fast was she going?
> F: I have no idea.
> S: Would you be willing to say that you reported the presence of this iceberg an hour before the collision?
> F: No sir.
> S: Forty-five minutes?
> F: No sir.
> S: A half an hour?
> F: No sir.
> S: Fifteen minutes?
> F: No sir.
> S: Ten minutes?
> F: No sir.
> S: How far was this 'black mass' when you first saw it?
> F: I have no idea sir.
> S: Can you give us some idea? Did it impress you as serious?

Fleet was getting bombarded by the questions and blurted out to a shocked audience, 'I reported it as soon as ever I seen it!' The senator changed tack and took a calmer approach to proceedings:

> S: How far an object was this when you first saw it?
> F: It was not very large when I first saw it.
> S: How large was it?
> F: I have no idea of distance and spaces.
> S: Was it as large as the table at which I am sitting?
> F: It would be as large as two tables put together when I first saw it.

Fleet, it appeared, was sticking fast to the story that had been given him by White Star Line representatives: there had been only one iceberg, a black mass, and no other ice had been seen. As a special lookout employed by the White Star Line, it appeared to Smith absurd that this man was claiming to have no idea of space and distances, however he was able to pick him up on this when questioned about his role in lifeboat 6. Smith asked Fleet about the arrival of the stowaway:

> S: When did you first see him?
> F: He was underneath the seat. We saw him as we got clear. He showed himself then.

S: As soon as you got clear? How far clear? Half a mile or so?

F: About a mile clear. We rested.

It seemed, therefore, that Fleet didn't have a problem with judging distance when he had left the crow's nest.

The senator could see that Fleet had been very nervous throughout his testimony. He was hiding something and Smith had not been able to get to the bottom of what it was. After further questioning about the missing binoculars and his time on the water, Senator Smith let Frederick Fleet step down.

Before the senator called any further crew members, he asked Major Arthur Peuchen to take the stand. Eyes had turned to him as being the only other male passenger to have been allowed into a lifeboat apart from Bruce Ismay. Peuchen must have realised how bad that would look to the hundreds of women whose husbands, brothers or fathers had been left behind. When Peuchen had been on *Carpathia* he had found Lightoller and asked him to sign a note to say that he had been ordered in by the second officer as there had not been enough men to man lifeboat 6. Lightoller had done so. Peuchen now gave a lengthy testimonial. He described how he had joined *Titanic* in Southampton and had been travelling with other gentlemen from Canada, none of whom had survived. He had been in the smoking room and had left to go to his cabin at around 11.20p.m. After the impact he had checked on his friends and, when he realised they were in a serious predicament, he had returned to his room to change and to put on heavy clothes and his lifejacket. He then went to the boat deck to assist with taking out sails and masts from the lifeboats and encouraging the women and children into the boats. He was very keen to tell the committee about a particular incident he had witnessed:

There was one act sir, I would like to mention, a little ahead of my story. When I came on deck first, on this upper deck, there were, it seemed to me, about 100 stokers who came up with their dunnage bags and they seemed to crowd this whole deck in front of the boats. One of the officers, I do not know which one but a very powerful one, came and drove these men right off that deck. It was a splendid act. He drove them, every man, like a lot of sheep, right off the deck.

The senator asked where these men had gone. 'I do not know. He drove them right ahead of him and they disappeared. I do not know where they went but it was a splendid act. They did not put up any resistance. I admired him for it,' the major replied.

Peuchen explained that he had helped remove tackle from a boat and was standing next to officer Lightoller by lifeboat 6 when a call came up for another seaman. Peuchen said, 'Can I be of assistance? I am a yachtsman and can handle a boat with the average man.' Lightoller had agreed and Peuchen had slid down the rope into the lifeboat. The major went on to testify that he'd had a row with Robert Hichens about changing places. He said Robert had sworn a lot and, when they suggested returning to the wreck site, said 'it is no use going back there, there are only a lot of stiffs,' which had upset the ladies in the boat a great deal. The senator wanted to know more about any further conversation between the major and Robert. 'Who was the quartermaster?' he asked. To which Peuchen replied:

> Hichen, spelt H.I.C.H.E.N. I think you can probably find him but he was the man at the wheel and he was calling out to other boats, wanting to know which officer was on watch that night. He did not seem to know which officer, at the time of sighting the iceberg, was on watch.

Peuchen added that he had asked Lightoller about this, and that the officer had said it was not always necessary for the bridge to respond to the crow's nest.

Peuchen told the committee how he had been rowing next to Fleet in the lifeboat and how they had been discussing the iceberg. 'What occurred?' Peuchen had asked the lookout man. In their conversation, he said Fleet rang three bells and he signalled to the bridge. The senator asked the major about this further:

> S: Did he say how far off the iceberg was when he first saw it?
> P: No, he did not go into that. The only thing he said was that he did not get a reply from the bridge.
> S: Did he tell you anything more about the iceberg and the collision than you have stated?
> P: No that is all.

Peuchen went on to repeat that the quartermaster had called over to other lifeboats to ask who the officer had been on the bridge. The senator clarified this:

S: To another lifeboat?
P: Yes.
S: What did he say?
P: I did not catch the answer, only that he didn't seem to know who was on duty when the ship struck.

There was another witness from lifeboat 6 who was to have a similar story to tell; one Mrs Lucien Smith. While on *Carpathia* she had been invited to use the cabin of a Mr and Mrs Hutchinson. Mrs Smith had told Mrs Hutchinson about her experiences and what she had heard, relaying that she blamed the captain for not having been on duty on the bridge. She said that three times the watch in the crow's nest had telephoned to the bridge that icebergs were in sight, but the captain was not there.

Senator Smith closed the hearing for the afternoon to resume the following morning, Tuesday 23 April. Fleet had been recalled but Smith had got no further with finding out what it was the lookout was trying to hide. He did not know who was responsible for keeping the man from the truth either. He had managed to subpoena a vital witness, Robert Hichens, the helmsman who would be testifying next, but first he wanted to make it absolutely clear that he would not stand for any further tampering of witness statements. When he stood up to address the participants, there was no doubt by the expression on his face the seriousness of what he had to say:

It is of course, very apparent that the surviving officers of the Titanic are not shipbuilders, having had nothing to do with the construction of that vessel and the Committee have assumed that if these witnesses should tell what they themselves know of the circumstances surrounding the ship up to the time of the collision and what transpired thereafter, this information would be about all that we could obtain from them.

One word as to the plan. It has been our intention from the beginning to first obtain the testimony of citizens or subjects of Great Britain who are temporarily in this country and this course will be pursued until the Committee conclude that they have obtained all information and useful and proper understanding of the disaster.

Misrepresentations have been made, I have heard. Personally, I have not seen a single newspaper since I was appointed Chairman of this Committee because I did not wish to be influenced by those papers or unduly encouraged. Neither did I wish to take on any partisan bias or prejudice whatsoever. The representatives of the press have all co-operated in every way possible to lighten the burden of the Committee and to assist in obtaining the results we seek.

At this point, Smith slammed his fist on the table:

The Committee will *not* tolerate any further attempt on the part of *anyone* to shape its course. We shall proceed in our own way, completing the official record and the judgements of our efforts may very appropriately be withheld until those who are disposed to question its wisdom have the actual official reports.

On the subject of not reading the newspapers, perhaps if he had, the senator would have discovered that there were many witnesses who had heard conversations on *Carpathia* about Frederick Fleet's early iceberg warnings, and the fact that his calls to the bridge were seemingly ignored. One witness, a steward called Thomas Whitely, was currently laid up in a New York hospital suffering the effects of exposure and frozen feet. Four different newspapers had been to interview him and all had reported a conversation he had heard between Reginald Lee and Frederick Fleet while on *Carpathia*. Although each newspaper ran a slightly different account in terms of wording and interpretation, what ran through all the articles was that the lookouts had started to see icebergs from 11.15p.m., and had warned the bridge on three separate occasions. They had appeared indignant that their warnings had been ignored, and Whitely was astonished and certain as to the last statement he had heard one of them say which was, 'No wonder Mr Murdoch shot himself'.

There had been different accounts of witnesses seeing officers shooting themselves. Eugene Daly, an Irish steerage passenger, had written to his sister directly after the sinking saying, 'I saw the officer shoot two men dead because they tried to get into a boat. Afterwards there was another shot and I saw the officer himself lying on the deck.' First-class passenger George Rheims wrote to his wife with a similar story:

> While the last boat was leaving, I saw an officer with a revolver fire a shot and kill a man who was trying to climb into it. As there remained nothing more to do, the officer told us, 'Gentlemen, each man for himself, good-bye'. He gave a military salute and then fired a bullet into his head. That's what I call a man!

Murdoch was the most senior officer on duty and in command of *Titanic* before the collision. He knew his career was ruined and that he was likely to face gross negligence charges and causing the deaths of 1,500 people. He had done all that he could to get as many people into lifeboats and away from the ship, but when the water began to run up to his knees, there was really only one course of action open to him.[35]

By the fifth day of the Inquiry many survivors had returned to their homes and it was becoming increasingly difficult to obtain statements from key eyewitnesses. When they were forthcoming, they appeared as affidavits. Mrs Catherine Crosby in hers wrote:

> It was reported on the 'Carpathia' by passengers whose names I do not recollect, that the lookout who was on duty at the time the Titanic struck the iceberg had said, 'I know they will blame me for it because I was on duty but it was not my fault. I had warned the officers three or four times before striking the iceberg that we were in the vicinity of icebergs but the officers on the bridge paid no attention to my signals'.

Returning from lunch recess on the fifth day, one of the most crucial witnesses to what had occurred on the night of Sunday 14 April was about to take the stand. Not only had he been steering *Titanic* at the time of the collision, but he would have seen and heard more than any other crew member surviving before, during and after the iceberg was sighted from his position in the wheelhouse. Moody, Murdoch and Captain Smith no longer had a voice. Quartermaster Robert Hichens took the stand and Senator Smith opened the questioning: 'I wish you would tell me now, in your own way, what happened that night from the time you went on watch until the collision occurred?' Robert replied:

I went on watch at 8 o'clock. The officers on the watch were
the second officer, Mr Lightoller, senior in command, the fourth
officer, Mr Boxhall and the sixth officer, Mr Moody. My first
orders when I got on the bridge was to take the second officer's
complements down to the ship's carpenter and inform him to
look to his fresh water, that it was about to freeze. I did so. On the
return to the bridge, it had been a couple of minutes when the
carpenter came back and reported the duty carried out. Standing
by, waiting for another message – it is the duty of the quartermaster to strike the bell every half hour – as the standby quartermaster
sir, I heard the second officer repeat to Mr Moody, the sixth
officer, to speak through the telephone, warning the lookout men
in the crow's nest to keep a sharp look out for small ice until
daylight and pass the word along to the other lookout men. The
next order I received from the second officer was to go and find
the deck engineer and bring up the key to open the heaters up
in the corridor of the officers' quarters, also in the wheelhouse
and the chartroom on account of the intense cold. At a quarter
to ten I called the first officer, Mr Murdoch, to let him know it
was one bell, which is part of our duty and also took the ther-
mometer and barometer, the temperature of the water and the
log. At 10 o'clock I went to the wheel sir. Mr Murdoch came
up to relieve Mr Lightoller. I had the course given me from the
other quartermaster, north 71 west which I repeated to him and
he went and reported it to the first officer or second officer in
charge which he repeated back – the course sir. All went along
very well until twenty minutes to twelve when three gongs come
from the lookout and immediately afterwards a report on the telephone 'iceberg right ahead'. The Chief Officer rushed from the
wing to the bridge, or I imagine so sir. Certainly I am enclosed in
the wheelhouse and I cannot see, only my compass. He rushed to
the engines. I heard the telegraph bell ring and also give the order,
'Hard-a-starboard,' with the sixth officer standing by me to see the
duty carried out and the quartermaster standing by my left side.
Repeated the order, 'Hard-a-starboard, the helm is hard over'.

Robert had told the committee the course of events leading up
to and including the collision. Not his course of events perhaps,
but the ones he had been 'drilled' on while on *Carpathia*. He
testified that he had seen on his course board that the ship had

Howard Humphreys

CLIENT.. JOB No............................... PAGE.......................

PROJECT... BY....................................... DATE.......................

SUBJECT.. CHECKED........................... DATE.......................

<u>COLLISION @ SEA.</u> (as requested)

(At NIGHT, No MOON, AT or close to FULL SPEED)

- HOW FAR CAN Anyone see on a dark night — ?
- What speed were the other ships doing ? —

MINIMUM REACTION TIME

6080 FT.
1 mile

0·36 N.MILES

SHIPS COURSE.

N.B. 4 MINUTES AT. 21·5 N.M/P.HR.

20°

= 0·36 × 4 min = 1·4 N.MILES.

REACTION TIME ESTIMATE.

Lookout SEES ICEBERG	0
CONFIRMS sighting	20 seconds
Energies Telephone	15 Seconds
Reports Iceberg	10 seconds
Officer Confirms message	5 Seconds
Confirms sighting	20 Seconds
Instructs Helmsman. To alter course	2. Seconds
Helmsman applies rudder	15 Seconds.
Ship begins to react to new Rudder position	10 Seconds

SAY. 5 N.MILE. TURNING CIRCLE @ Speed.

SCALE. 1 MILE

1,216 Feet

REACTION TIME ASSUMING   97 Seconds

THAT THERE IS NO DELAY.

DISTANCE TRAVELLED   0·36 NAUTICAL MILES.

John Chittenden 3./Oct/2010

Diagram of the time *Titanic* had to avoid iceberg. (John Chitenden) veered two points to port as a result of him turning the wheel. Fleet had also testified that the ship had moved 'two points'. But had it? This part of *Titanic* history is one of the most debated and argued about. Trials after the sinking on *Titanic*'s sister ship *Olympic* showed that it would have taken 37 seconds for the ship to have turned two points at the speed she was going. Would this really have been enough time from when the ice was seen and instructions were given to the helmsman and the engine room, for the manoeuvre to be carried out successfully? Or had this information been fed to the remaining crew in a vain attempt to show that efforts had been made to avoid hitting the iceberg? John Chittenden, former naval officer on ships comparable to the size of *Titanic*, provided me with his calculations as to how long it would have taken *Titanic* to turn and he estimated 97 seconds.

Robert went on to testify that he was relieved at the wheel with the order to get the boats out, which he did, being subsequently put in command of lifeboat 6. He told how they were to pull for a light but that no matter how far they rowed, it moved further away. He said the ladies in the boat were in a bad way and very nervous but some of them had taken up oars. Robert told how he had eventually tied up to another boat and had been given a fireman to help with the rowing. Robert emphatically denied that he had refused to go back for survivors at the request of passengers in the boat. The reason he had not gone back was firstly because of the suction, and secondly because when she went down they were about a mile away. It was pitch black, he had no compass and could not tell where the cries were coming from. He and the other boats around him had been calling to each other and showing each other their lights and had all been in the same position. When asked who had given him the order to row for a light and offload passengers, Robert replied that it had been the first or second officer, he was not sure which. The senator asked Robert about the conditions:

> S: Did you have any way of your own by which you knew whether you were in the vicinity of icebergs?
>
> R: It began to get very cold, exceedingly cold, so cold we could hardly suffer the cold. I thought then there was ice about, some-where.
>
> S: That indicated that you were in the vicinity of ice?

R: It did not concern me. It had nothing to do with me at all. The officers had to do with it. I am only a junior officer.

Robert had read in the papers what some of the women had said about him in the lifeboat and had heard the rumours of him being a bully and a coward; he was now not going to leave the stand without speaking out for his own protection. When Senator Smith made ready to excuse Robert and asked the quartermaster if there was anything further he wished to say, Robert composed himself and said:

I would like to make a little statement as regarding Mrs Meyer's article in the newspapers about my drinking the whisky sir and about the blankets. I was very cold sir and I was standing up in the boat. I had no hat on. A lady had a flask of whisky or brandy, or something of that description, given her by some gentleman on the ship before she left and she pulled it out and gave me about a teaspoon and I drank it. Another lady, who was lying in the bottom of the boat in a rather weak condition gave me a half wet, half dry blanket to try to keep myself warm as I was half frozen. I think it was very unkind of her sir, to make any statement criticising me. When we got to the ship I handled everyone as carefully as I could and I was the last one to leave the boat and I do not think I deserve anything like that to be put in the papers. That is what upset me and got on my nerves.

The senator had no more questions for Robert and seemed satisfied that he had given a full account. He gave him permission to leave and return to the *Celtic* which was leaving New York the following day for Liverpool.

Charles Lightoller was beginning to feel the strain of the Inquiry. He had been recalled and seemed to be spending the whole time defending and protecting the White Star Line. He even testified that it was he who had persuaded Bruce Ismay to send the messages about holding the *Cedric* to take the crew home without setting foot on US soil. The reason for this, he explained, was not because he believed there would be an inquiry in New York, but because if the crew landed at port they would disappear to find other work on other ships in order to earn money for their families back home, especially the quartermasters who were so valued by other ships' masters. Lightoller maintained that throughout the evacuation there had been absolute calm and no panic at all, although other witnesses had testified to shots being fired to control the crowds desperately trying to escape the sinking ship, and of hundreds of people clinging on to the stern as it came out of the water only to slide down the decks or drop 70ft into the water below – where hundreds more were screaming and dying as the lifeboats rowed away. He went on to say that he had seen William Murdoch working at freeing a lifeboat, 'a hero right up until the end', even though his position on the other side of the deck would have made it impossible for him to have seen this. Lightoller also wrote to Murdoch's wife telling her the story, perhaps to spare her from the terrible rumours of her husband's suicide. In attempting to protect his employer, however, what Lightoller had in fact done was tie himself up in knots, and without realising it had damaged the reputation of the White Star Line – a misdeed that would not go unpunished as he would never command a ship belonging to White Star Line.

The Inquiry would continue in Washington and then back in New York for nearly two more weeks. There were two cases that the senator had a particular interest in. One concerned the ice warnings: the messages that had been sent to *Titanic* on the night of Sunday 14th by other ships and the Hydrographic Office. The other seemed fantastic, but potentially important enough that Smith had made a decision to follow it up. A call had come through from the Austro-Hungarian ambassador, Baron Hengelmuller, from the consulate in Cleveland, Ohio. Hengelmuller was currently holding a Hungarian sailor called Luis Klein on a charge of mutiny. (The charge of mutiny must have been for leaving his ship in New York, although this charge was later dropped.) He was in a very agitated frame of mind and, although unwell, was desperate to give information about what he had witnessed while acting as ordinary seaman aboard *Titanic*. With the help of an interpreter the sailor sat through a gruelling cross-examination by federal officials and would not budge from his story. He alleged he had seen a party going on in one of the cabins, with wine being passed around, and officers and other members of the crew had been drinking and getting intoxicated. He went on to say that he had also seen the officer of the watch asleep on deck. Moreover, he would willingly go to Washington and point out to the committee the members of the crew he had seen by sight.

Senator Smith had heard enough rumours circulating about intemperance and had learned a great deal about the lavish banquet that had been held for the captain's retirement celebrations. Although the claims of this sailor appeared far-fetched, his gut feeling was to see what he had to say for himself in front of the committee. In Cleveland, Deputy United States Marshall Charles Morgan had the job of escorting Klein down by train to Washington. Before they left, Klein had signed a process order, which read:

> Office of the United States Attorney
> Northern District of Ohio
> Cleveland, Ohio, Monday April 22nd, 1912
> Gentlemen: I hereby waive issuance and service of process and subpoena on me in the matter of the investigation of the so-called Titanic disaster, before the United States Senate sub-committee and voluntary consent to be taken by the United States Marshall from Cleveland, Ohio to Washington D.C. for the purpose of giving my testimony before said Committee.

They arrived on Tuesday morning, but before Morgan arranged for Klein to be accommodated in a nearby hotel he took him to the office of Senator Smith to sign him in as a witness. While he had been at the senator's office, someone else had seen him there – Charles Herbert Lightoller. Although Morgan was to tell the senator later in front of the committee that he had attempted to look after Klein during his stay and had seen him up until 11p.m. on the Tuesday evening, by 7a.m. the following morning, Klein had disappeared. Apparently witnessed by a hotel staff member, Luis Klein had departed from the hotel. Morgan had gone to his room and found that he had left all his belongings, including his collar and necktie.

On Saturday 27 April, Senator Smith once again called Lightoller to the stand and questioned him:

> S: Mr Lightoller. Are you familiar with the ship's crew of the Titanic when she left Southampton and at the time of the accident?
> L: You are speaking of the seamen are you?

S:Yes.

L:Yes sir.

S: Have you ever known Luis Klein?

L: Not among the seamen.

S:Was there such a member of the crew of the Titanic?

L: I am given to understand that there was one man named Klein who was a second class barber. That man is personally known to me. He is the only Klein who was on board so far as I know.

S: Did he survive?

L: He did not.

Senator Smith then asked Lightoller who the principal barber was on board the ship. Lightoller had forgotten his name but believed he hadn't survived. When further pressed, and on consulting a memorandum he had on his person, Lightoller realised that in fact he had survived and that he was the only American crew member on board by the name of 'Whitman' or 'Whiteman' (it was in fact 'Weikman'). He apologised profusely for the misunderstanding.

In an affidavit the man in question, August Weikman, had testified that he had been standing on the starboard side and had reportedly seen Chief Officer Wilde 'order' Bruce Ismay into collapsible boat C. He went on to say that he believed Ismay was justified in getting aboard the lifeboat – why he would believe that is unclear. Interestingly, Lightoller had also made an earlier testimony that while on the *Carpathia* he had heard from a reliable source (was it Weikman?) the following information:

It is that Chief Officer Wilde was at the starboard boat in which Bruce Ismay went away and that he told Mr Ismay, 'There are no more women on board the ship'. Wilde was a pretty big, powerful chap and he was a man that would not argue very long. Mr Ismay was right there. Naturally he was there close to the boat because he was working at the boats and he was working the collapsible boat and that is why he was there and Mr Wilde, who was near him, simply bundled him into the boat.

Lightoller went on to say that he believed what he had been told by 'the source' was the truth.

Bruce Ismay testified that no one had ordered him into a boat and that he had gone on his own when he could see no further women on the deck. Quartermaster Rowe who was at the same end of the lifeboat and could hear and see everything, also testified that no one had ordered Ismay in and that he got in of his own accord. It appeared that both Lightoller and Weikman were trying to protect Ismay by saying that he was ordered into the lifeboat. Further investigation showed that Weikman was a first-class barber, unusual in that he was American, who had served with the White Star Line for thirty-four years, and so would have been well known among the crew. He had been another witness to seeing Murdoch shoot someone, as he later reported in the *Daily Enterprise* on 20 April.

Senator Smith continued to question Lightoller over the crew:

> S: Did you see a man here in my office this week who claimed
> to be Luis Klein, a surviving member of the crew of the Titanic?
> L: I believe that I did sir.
> S: Had you ever seen him before?
> L: Never.

Smith asked Lightoller if he knew who had made up the list of the surviving members of crew when they were on *Carpathia*. Lightoller replied that he had gone through the list himself with the help of chief second-class steward John Hardy.

Luis Klein had indeed left his hotel suddenly. He would turn up a year later in Little Venice, California. Described by local businessmen as an entrepreneur, he ran a concession on the Windward Pier, a theatrical production known for its 'wonderful representation of the sinking of the Titanic'. Two years later he would run another show about the *Lusitania*, which opened just a couple of days after that disaster. How did Luis Klein get from being a low-ranking ordinary seaman to an entrepreneur able to set himself up in California? A man so determined to point the finger at drunken officers in front of a senate committee was now re-enacting his experience in front of a very different audience that wanted to hear his story. Where did he get the money to set himself up? Had he been paid for his silence? If so, by whom? Research has so far shown that Luis Klein does not appear on the crew records. There were of course anomalies on the records – name changes and the like, and also the problems with crew changes in the particulars of engagement. That being the case, how would the White Star Line have reacted knowing that this man was on his way to Washington, desperate to point the finger at drunk officers? Another mystery that may perhaps never be solved.[36]

During the *Titanic* inquiry, Senator Smith had struggled with the seemingly cavalier way the ship's captain and officers had sailed carelessly at full speed into waters that were infested with just about every type of ice. Especially considering other ships had sent *Titanic* at least four warnings before she had finally collided with a 'lone' iceberg. Not being a nautical man or an expert in the subject of ice movements in the north Atlantic, Smith would now call on a man who he believed could answer the questions that had been bugging him for more than two weeks. John Knapp was the Hydrographer of the Bureau of Navigation, Navy Department, Washington DC. The Bureau's task was to help improve the means of safe navigation of the seas by providing nautical charts, as well as collecting all kinds of information relating to sea conditions, for the benefit of the seamen whose responsibility it was to navigate as part of their maritime marine responsibilities. The observations would come in the form of letters or radio messages transmitted ship-to-shore or ship-to-ship, providing an invaluable aid for seafarers. It would be down to the seamen of a particular vessel to estimate the speed and direction of any obstructions they may encounter with the use of their charts.

Knapp explained that prior to 14 April, the Hydrographic Office had received numerous reports of ice in the north Atlantic. The steamship *Amerika* had reported two large icebergs in latitude 41°, 27' N, longitude 50°, 8' W (*Titanic* had foundered at latitude 41° 46' N, longitude 50° 14' W), and this message had been received by *Titanic* at 13.45p.m. Knapp produced a chart which he showed to the committee, outlining the reports made by various steamers at around the same time as *Titanic* had gone down. He especially wanted the committee to see the report from the *Mesaba* in latitude 42° N, longitude 50° W, at 2p.m. on Sunday 14 April. The report read, 'passed another field of pack ice with numerous bergs intermixed and extended from four points on the starboard bow to abeam on the port side. Had to steer 20 miles south to clear it.' This ice was reported as being directly in the track to which *Titanic* was heading when she met with her accident.

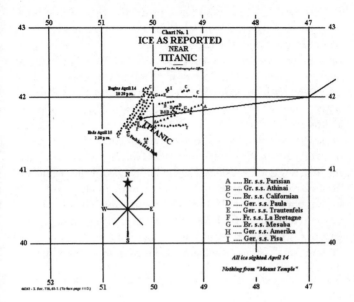

Ice chart. (Titanic Inquiry Project)

The steamship *Baltic* similarly reported ice to *Titanic*, which was acknowledged by Captain Smith at 11.05a.m. on the Sunday. That same evening, a further report had come through from the *Californian* which was stuck in field ice just miles from where *Titanic* sank. Many believed she was the steamship which *Titanic* had seen on the port bow and which had not replied to their lamp messages for help. Captain Lord of the *Californian* would be blamed for decades to come by those who were sure he had ignored the rescue calls from the stricken liner.

The US Inquiry was finally coming to an end. Following eighteen days of hearings with eighty-six witnesses and 1,000 pages of testimony given, Senator Smith and his committee had failed to find one person or one cause directly responsible for the loss of *Titanic*. What Smith had done, however, was to record for history the witness statements of some of those who had survived and had come to tell what they had seen just days before. But still, of the eighty-six crew and passengers who had given statements, what of the remaining men and women from the 705 survivors who hadn't taken the stand and had their own harrowing stories to tell?

There was one man who never made it to the stand in New York or Washington, a man who was a crucial witness but who had been missed by the committee and detained in New York on the *Celtic*: the other lookout and Frederick Fleet's mate in the crow's nest, Reginald Lee. There was a reason why the White Star Line may not have wanted Lee to take the stand. He had previously been discharged from the Royal Navy in disgrace for being a chronic alcoholic, which led to medical treatment for *delirium tremens* (severe alcohol withdrawal), an affliction of a very heavy drinker. Perhaps his service record was missing when he signed on. Still, it was an oversight that the shipping company would no doubt have wanted to keep very much to themselves. Although he was absent at the US Inquiry, he was later called to appear before the Board of Trade Wreck Commission and an important part of his testimony would shed a 'hazy' but at the same time 'illuminating' picture of what he had seen in the minutes before disaster struck.

11

⟻⧾ HOMECOMING ⧾⟼

It was Tuesday 16 April and a sign had been put up in the window at the *Sunday Times* offices in Southampton. It read, 'The Titanic has sunk!' The words flew like wildfire around the city and Florence Hichens would no doubt have joined the steady flow which turned into a crowd of other wives and mothers, hurrying down to the White Star Line offices in Canute Road just up from the dock gates; everyone in total disbelief that this could have happened. When they arrived there was no news, only rumours: *Titanic* was being towed to Halifax, all saved; no, the ship went down, all lost; many drowned, others saved. The uncertainty was agony. It was the not knowing that quickly turned the initial shock into blind panic, and women started running all over the place, knocking on doors, pouncing upon any official-looking person; angry at the officials whose heads were shaking and shoulders shrugging as they made hasty retreats before the crowd's questions turned into violent threats.

There were no lists up and no one was telling them anything. The crowd waited but as it started getting dark those mothers with young children had to go home. There would be many who would not leave their spot all night. Florence must have felt sick for not wanting to hear dreadful tidings, but soon there was news: returning to the White Star Line offices the following day, scores of people crowded around the huge signs that had been put up, clearly showing the names of those saved. Ball, Bennett, Combes, Ellis, Fitzpatrick, Gibbons, Harris, Hebb, Hichens. He was on the list! For Florence there was huge relief but many others were not so lucky. How could anyone bear to listen as the cries started and screams came from the women who had got bad news? How they must have felt for their loved ones being alive, while others were dead or missing.

Northam had been the worst hit, with almost every family having lost a son, father or brother; sometimes more than one member. All the blinds were pulled down and what had only two days before been a noisy, bustling city fell into the shattering silence of mourning. Flags flew at half-mast on every civic build-ing. There were no children in the street, just a cold wind blowing flakes of late spring snow, which collected in the gutters for a day and then was gone. Six hundred families had lost relatives, creating social hardships for those left behind. (Southampton would also lose 2,000 men in the First World War.) In the next few days, as the city tried to come to terms with what had happened, a tel-egram came with the official news that Robert was safe, as did the money order that would see them through until his return. It would be two weeks before Florence would see Robert again. On Sunday 28 April the Red Star Line ship *Lapland* was waiting outside the dock at Plymouth with 200 survivors. The remaining survivors were displaced in New York. Robert, meanwhile, would be arriving in Liverpool on the *Celtic* on 4 May with some of the other crew who had been excused from the US Inquiry. The offic-ers and Bruce Ismay would return later on the *Adriatic*. Robert's group would be heading down to London and put up in digs in Whitechapel in readiness for their second bout of questioning in front of the Board of Trade.

Back in Plymouth, security was intense with policemen in the port erecting cordons to keep journalists away from the survivors. The cordons, however, kept anxious relatives and friends from seeing their loved ones too. Board of Trade and White Star officials were waiting for the *Lapland*, making it quite clear that until state-ments had been taken from every one of the crew for the British Inquiry, they would be detained in waiting rooms near the dock gates, with dining rooms and sleeping arrangements made ready. Representatives from the Seafarers Union approached the *Lapland* by tender, asking to speak to the crew. The White Star Line refused them access and when the crew found out they warned that they would not give any statements to anyone unless they could speak to their union. Eventually they were allowed on board and the liner made its way to the dock. During the next twenty-four hours 138 crew gave written statements telling of their experiences of the disaster. Not one of these dispositions was ever made public and did not appear as evidence at the British Inquiry. They were lost or destroyed, containing what must have been valuable narratives. Finally, when the officials had finished with the exhausted crew, they were allowed to leave and return to their grateful relatives crowding behind the gates outside.[37]

The London Scottish Drill Hall would be the setting for the Board of Trade Wreck Inquiry into the sinking of *Titanic*. Commissioner Lord Mersey presided over the hearings with Sir Rufus Isaacs representing the Board of Trade, who were the very Government ministry that had agreed on the insignificant number of lifeboats on the ship and were responsible for other antiquated maritime safety laws. Unlike the US Inquiry which had been sorely lacking in nautical experts, the British hearings were full of them. Even so, over the next twenty-eight days many of the same questions would be asked and the same answers given, with a few interesting exceptions. At this inquiry both the lookouts, Frederick Fleet and Reginald Lee, were present, but somehow their testimonies had altered and they couldn't quite manage to agree on what the other was saying. In addition, at the US Inquiry, the overriding description of the conditions that night from witnesses was that it was perfectly clear and starlit with excellent visibility. During Charles Lightoller's discussion with the captain at 9p.m. they had spoken on this very topic in some detail, and only when the commander left the bridge did he leave instructions to be called immediately if the conditions changed, and that if there was any haze they were to go very slowly. There was no mention of any haze developing at all on that night when questioned in America, but the case seemed slightly different once back in England.

Reginald Lee was one of the first to take the stand. The attorney general asked Lee general questions about his service at sea, his duties as lookout and the message sent up from Sixth Officer Moody about the small ice and growlers:

AG: What sort of night was it?
L: A clear, starry night overhead but at the time of the accident

there was a haze right ahead.

AG: At the time of the accident there was a haze ahead?

L: A haze right ahead – in fact it was extending more or less round the horizon.

AG: Did you notice this haze which extended on the horizon when you first came on watch, or did it come later?

L: It was not so distinct then, not to be noticed but we had our work cut out to pierce through it after we started. My mate [Fleet] happened to pass the remark to me, 'well, if we can see through this we'll be lucky'. That was when we began to notice there was a haze on the water.

When asked what the iceberg looked like, Lee answered that it was a dark mass that came through the haze, one side of it was black but as it passed, the other side was white and it had a white fringe on top. This was interesting because when Lightoller later came to testify, he had added much more to the already elaborate conversation he had allegedly had with the captain, and what he had told the Inquiry in America. When asked what the conditions were like and what was said between him and the commander, Lightoller's new testimony was:

> I remember saying, 'In any case, there will be a certain amount of reflected lights from the bergs' to which the Captain agreed, then we both agreed that even if the blue side of a berg was towards us, probably the outline would give us sufficient warning, that we should be able to see it at good distance. Of course it was just with regards to that possibility of the blue side being towards us and if it did happen to be turned towards us, there would still be a white outline.

So with no mention of blue-sided icebergs with white outlines or fringes or impenetrable hazes in America, they appeared out of nowhere in England (rather like the iceberg). The attorney general continued to question Lee on his role in helping with the lifeboats *et al.* and then excused him. He wanted to see what the other lookout had to say. When Fleet took the stand the man who had previously sworn to a perfectly clear night with excellent vision, even without binoculars, now had a different picture to paint. Still very nervous, he had to contend with Bruce Ismay and Charles Lightoller practically boring holes in the side of his head with their steely stares. The attorney general asked Fleet about the conditions:

AG: Now, at the time you went in the crow's nest, was the sky clear?

F: Yes.

AG: The sea we know was very calm?

F: Yes.

AG: The stars were shining?

F: Yes.

AG: Could you clearly see the horizon?

F: The first part of the watch we could.

AG: After the first part of the watch, what was the change if anything?

F: A sort of slight haze.

AG: A slight haze?

F: Yes.

AG: Was the haze on the waterline?

F: Yes.

AG: It prevented you from seeing the horizon clearly?

F: It was nothing to talk about.

AG: Was this haze ahead of you?

F: Well, it was about two points on each side.

Fleet repeated that the haze was nothing much to speak of and didn't affect their vision at all. He was then reminded of Lee's testimony: 'My mate [Fleet] said, "if we can see through this we will be lucky".' To which Fleet quickly replied, 'I never said that!' 'You never said that?' asked the attorney general. 'No,' came the definite answer. The commissioner was of the opinion that Lee had invented the haze to make any excuse for not seeing the iceberg in time. Was that exactly what Charles Lightoller wanted him to think?

When Robert took the stand on the third day, he was asked almost the same set of questions as in America. The commissioner persistently asked him why he hadn't returned for survivors but Robert stayed with his facts, that there was no compass, total darkness and no way of knowing, almost a mile away, which direction he should go. Although the Board of Trade wanted to find someone responsible, at the end of both investigations no one had got to the bottom of how *Titanic* had sunk. Blame was apportioned to her speed, freakish weather conditions and missed ice warnings; to the over confidence of the captain and the ignorance of the officers and badly trained crew. Not enough lifeboats, missing binoculars and insufficient lookouts added to the list of incompetence.

There appear to be many things the inquiries overlooked, however. Why, for example, had there been no mention of Murdoch's movements between 10p.m. and 11.40p.m., the moment of impact? There was a complete void of information in that one hour and forty minutes' time span. Where was the captain during this critical time? What time had Boxhall and Moody left the bridge area? There was no record of conversations between the officers or the quartermasters, no real evidence of charts being discussed or courses checked; just a vagueness at a time when the ship was clearly due to reach the ice region. Only a tenuous remark from Robert, the man at the helm: 'All went along very well until twenty minutes to twelve.' The silence over these matters instead spoke volumes. Lightoller's expertise at evading and batting back questions, the other officers' whereabouts, and the party line that had clearly been given Fleet, Lee and Robert: all these lies and excuses were missed and washed over as the commissioners searched in the wrong places.

If they had perhaps spent more time getting to the bottom of what the crucial witnesses actually saw and heard they may have found the truth. If so many of the other important witnesses could have told their stories, perhaps they would have got there in the end, but they didn't. If the first officer, William Murdoch, had been at his post, on watch and meticulously scanning the horizon for the known dangers ahead, *Titanic* would perhaps not have steamed into an iceberg that most people agreed was big and white and hard and iceberg shaped – like all the other icebergs ships had reported and the survivors said they had seen in the area the following morning. Expert witnesses had even told how they believed a blue/black iceberg was incredibly rare. If there had been more lookouts stationed on the bridge or around the ship at a time when *Titanic* was known to be reaching the ice region, the collision may not have occurred. While Fleet and Lee stuck to their duty as special lookouts, and Robert held the wheel and took his orders for as long as he felt he could, there remained the one awful conclusion. According to the Thomas Garvey letter, Robert had shouted in Murdoch's ear but couldn't wake him – why? Because Murdoch was out cold from the wine he had consumed at a celebration for his captain? It had been freezing on the outer bridge, maybe he had just sat down out of the cold for a minute and with the heaters fired up, he had fallen asleep.

Whether the rule laid down by White Star was total temperance among the crew or not, this night had been an exception, a special occasion, and whether the officers had drunk one sip or three glasses of wine, the evidence points to the fact that in all probability they did. The rules were broken and in the end human error, or gross negligence depending on your view, was to blame for the death of 1,500 people. White Star Line had essentially gotten away with murder, as it was the shipping company who were ultimately responsible for the *Titanic*. All White Star Line had to do now was to keep the secret by silencing the key witnesses, of which there were few, and the only way they needed to do that was with the promise of employment and financial support for as long as their mouths were kept shut.

So what happened to the surviving officers and also to the crew who had been on duty at the time of the disaster? Quartermasters Rowe and Olliver, Frederick Fleet and Officers Pitman, Lightoller and Boxhall all continued working for the White Star Line. Officer Lowe, who had worked for different shipping companies and on many different types of vessel before *Titanic*, returned to his home town with a hero's welcome for picking up survivors and continued his career on the sea. Lee was found dead in his bedroom at a sailor's home in Southampton, one year after the sinking. His death certificate read heart disease with complications, although Fleet believed his mate had gone back to hard drinking after his experience, as he was to tell Leslie Reade, author of *The Ship that Stood Still*, many years later.

But what about Robert Hichens?

12

‘SPIRITED AWAY’

Robert finally returned to his family soon after he had testified. The joy of being reunited with them was mixed with sadness; so many families in the streets around his had lost their loved ones. He had known some of those men from the area and it would have been heart-rending to meet those left behind in the street. What words could he say? Although he had only been following orders, it was known that he had been at the wheel and word spread fast. Sailors were superstitious and would no doubt see Robert as bad luck. Meanwhile his family in Newlyn had been frantic with worry until they received word that their son had survived. Robert's father Phillip, in reply to the news he had received, wrote:

My Dear Daughter,

In answer to your letter and postcard which I have now received thanking God for the good news of my dear boy. We know he was saved this morning and we were waiting for news. Oh the tears that have been shed here God only knows. No rest only from this morning then the tears of joy. Poor mother took to her to bed just after the letter came. Could not get her to eat anything. She seen Robert on Sunday morning about one o'clock with his two daughters up in the air and waked me and I said she was dreaming. She says no, she was wide awake.

There was one duty Robert could perform on behalf of a friend he had made on *Titanic* who came from the Isle of White. Robert took the train to Portsmouth and then the short ferry journey over to the island. He went to the home of the parents of William Cheverton, who had been a first-class steward. The twenty-seven-year-old had died in the sinking but his body had been recovered. Robert spent some time telling his family of their short friendship and what they had talked about earlier in the day before the tragedy. When he left them to return to Southampton he was stopped by journalists who wanted to cover his story, and he spoke to them and had his picture taken by the memorial in the square. He told the *Hampshire Independent*, which came out on 1 June, about his experiences in the lifeboat and about how they had been the last to reach *Carpathia* after seven hours at sea. He told them that the captain was on the bridge right up until the last and how, like everyone, he had thought *Titanic* was unsinkable. Robert finally added that he thought that some of the questions asked in America had been absurd and that the British Inquiry was far more intelligible.

Now that Robert had finished giving evidence he would have to think of his future employment. What reward would the White Star Line give to Robert for standing up in two inquiries and lying for his employers? Another posting as quartermaster? Probably not, perhaps an able seaman's job on a smaller liner, or even a desk job like Frederick Fleet? No. Robert would be seen as an embarrassment for the shipping line and it would be too risky for him to be hovering around where he might 'accidentally' say the wrong thing to the wrong person. The Thomas Garvey letter states that Robert was 'given a lifelong job with good pay for as long as he remained silent'. It would be easy for the White Star Line to pull strings and get him a berth on a ship, any ship, as long as it was one that took him a long way away. So before long Robert left for South Africa, and for the next ten years or so he almost seemed to disappear. Before he left England, Robert was able to enjoy the arrival of his third daughter, Phyllis May, in July and spent a few weeks with his family before he was 'spirited away'.

In 1914 very little was done to help victims of disaster in the way of psychological support. It was very much the generation of 'stiff upper lip' and a 'pull yourself together man' attitude. Robert kept himself working and served on a number of vessels between 1912–14 including the *Maxwelton*, *Soudan*, *Ruban* and *Norah James*, but with being away for long periods with rare visits back home his mental wellbeing began to suffer. Not surprising, really, when you consider what he had been through. He had been vilified as a bully and a coward in the newspapers in New York. Superstitious crewmen saw him as jinxed and didn't want to sail with him. His unblemished twelve-year career since 1900 counted for nothing. He had witnessed a terrible tragedy and heard the sound of hundreds of people dying. He had failed his religion as a liar and was bottling up a huge secret. He needed to get things off his chest before he went stark raving mad.

It was while he was in Cape Town early in 1914 that Robert finally had an opportunity to unburden himself of his troubles. A British ship had come into port and on it was a quartermaster called Henry Blum, who had served on many White Star Line ships. Robert felt as though he could trust him enough to tell him what had really happened on *Titanic*. He swore Henry to secrecy for ten years and then told him how he had heard the lookouts warning of ice and had tried to wake the first officer who had had found on the lounger in the pilothouse. He told him that he and others had been virtually held under house arrest when they got back to England, and about being silenced by the White Star Line. Henry did keep the vow and Robert must have felt some temporary relief for sharing his secret. The men parted and Robert continued to work on land and at sea until he returned to England when he was needed as in the summer of 1914 the First World War broke out.

Before Robert left for the barracks in Portsmouth where he would be stationed, he once again spent a pitifully short period of time with Florence, Edna, Frances, Phyllis and his first son, Robert (Bob), who had been conceived and born the previous year. This was the life that many wives and husbands had to endure; they just had to make the best of things. Robert was mustered on 2 August 1914. The primary role of the Portsmouth barracks was to supply men for warships. Robert's accommodation was on the famous ship, HMS *Victory*, which was berthed permanently in Portsmouth Harbour. In the first few weeks of the war the place was a hive of activity. Robert joined in with the training and many of the activities put on for the men: boxing, football and keeping physically fit. They were also entertained by concerts and cinema shows which were popular with all the men. Over the next few months Robert's conduct was recorded as very good, and in body he was ready to mobilise when his time came. In spirit, however, he was having a hard time. When unusual symptoms led him to be examined by the company doctor at the barracks, he was diagnosed with neurasthenia. The symptoms of this nervous disorder included chest pains, panic attacks, chronic fatigue and anxiety. In 1914 neurasthenia, shell shock and battle fatigue were conditions normally associated with trauma, often leading the victim into alcoholism and in some cases violent behaviour. Post-traumatic stress disorder would not be recognised as a condition for many years, however the symptoms Robert displayed at this time showed some similarity. Although Robert had been promoted to leading seaman and would receive his British War Medal during his enlistment, his condition meant that he was invalided out of the Reserves.

Robert returned to a life of obscurity for the next fifteen years. In 1915, another daughter, Ivy Doreen (who would be called 'Babe') was born. Robert spent time in Hong Kong and brought back beautiful gifts for his children. Rumour had it in the family that he had been gun running in China, up the Yangtze River. He was able to provide for his family and, in 1924, Robert and Florence decided to leave Southampton and go back to Torquay. Ten years after Babe had been born, Florence gave birth to their final child, Frederick, in 1925. The Hichens' daughters remained in Southampton to marry or start families of their own. Florence was very close to her sister Beatrice and together they ran a guest house in the wealthy area of Warbury.

At forty-seven Robert had spent many years out on the open ocean and now settled in Torquay, wanting to find a way to earn money closer to home on land. Being such a popular seaside town he invested in a motor launch called the *Queen Mary* with the savings he had accrued during his time at sea. The problem was, he bought it from a man with a bad reputation for being a troublemaker and a shark, and Robert was about to head for some very big trouble indeed.

...ip and Rebecca Hichens. (Private collection)

Robert Hichens. (From Seamna's Card, Southampton Library)

Two of Robert's brothers: top left William,
bottom left Sidney. (Private collection)

Robert's sister, Juliette.

st's impression of Primrose Court in St Peter's Square. (Rick Parsons)

eter's Square before slum clearance. (Pam Lomax, Newlyn Archive Centre)

Florence Mortimore. (Private collection)

Young Freddie peering out of the hotel window where Florence worked, *c.*1930. (Private collection)

Doreen (Babe). (Private collection)

The district in which the Hichens lived in Southampton. (Southampton Heritage Collection)

Titanic officers Lowe, Lightoller, Boxhall and Pitman (seated). (Maritime Quest)

Titanic officers William Murdoch, Henry Wilde, Joseph Boxhall and Captain Smith. (Maritime Quest)

Lifeboat 6 with Robert standing at the tiller. (US National Archives)

Right: Titanic takes to the water.

Left: Margaret Tobin Brown, later to be christened the 'unsinkable Molly Brown'. (Maritime Quest)

SHIPWRECKED CREW OF S. S. *TITANIC*

ic crew at a memorial service in New York. Top right and four down with the light cap is Reginald
nd Robert Hichens is standing to the left of Reginald. (Southampton Heritage Collection)

Two Witnesses in Titanic Hearing Before Committee at Capitol

C. H. LIGHTHOLLER,
Second officer of the Titanic, who testified before Senate Committee.

ROBERT HICHENS.
Titanic's quartermaster allowed to return to England after testifying.

Artist's impression at *Titanic* Inquiry of Charles Lightoller and Robert Hichens.
(Encyclopaedia Titanica)

Left: Artist's impression of Robert Hichens at the Titanic Inquiry. (Encyclopedia Titanica)

Below: Lookout Frederick Fleet. (Maritime Quest)

rt Hichens on the Isle of Wight having visited the parents of William Cheverton.
hampton Heritage Collection)

ert and Reginald Lee in Liverpool after returning on the *Celtic*. Robert is far left, Lee far
. (Southampton Heritage Collection)

Robert's youngest son, Freddie. (Private collection)

Phyllis Hichens, '*Titanic* Baby'. (Private collection)

Phyllis, Florence and Frances Hichens. (Private collection)

Frances wearing a Kimono brought back from the orient while her partner Percy was in the Royal Navy.

Robert's eldest daughter Edna. (Private collection)

ons of Phyllis Hichens: James, Graham, Warner and Bev. (Private collection)

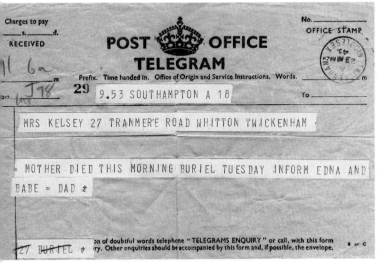

Charges to pay

____s.____d.

RECEIVED

No.____

OFFICE STAMP

POST ✦ OFFICE
TELEGRAM

Prefix. Time handed in. Office of Origin and Service Instructions. Words.____

29   9.53 SOUTHAMPTON A 18

To____

MRS KELSEY 27 TRANMERE ROAD WHITTON TWICKENHAM =

= MOTHER DIED THIS MORNING BURIEL TUESDAY INFORM EDNA AND

BABE = DAD +

27 BURIEL +

on of doubtful words telephone " TELEGRAMS ENQUIRY " or call, with this form
ry. Other enquiries should be accompanied by this form and, if possible, the envelope.

B or C

elegram Robert sent in Southampton telling of Florence's death. (Private collection)

Florence and Robert in Torquay in happier times. The woman on Robert's left arm is thought to be Florence's sister, Beatrice.

13

HARRY HENLEY

Robert bought the *Queen Mary* in 1930 for £160 from a man named Harry Henley. Harry wanted to sell the launch because he had got into a row with the other boatmen and had been ordered out of the gardens – the place where the launches departed. Robert paid Harry £100 in cash with an agreement to pay the remaining £60 over the following two years. Although the season started well the country was on the brink of the terrible depression of the 1930s, and in the spring of 1931 his business dried up completely. Robert had borrowed money from a Mr Squires in Torquay, but with no money coming in he was under pressure to pay him back. Robert described Harry as a mean man who began threatening him constantly and saying he would get a writ ordered on him if he didn't get his money. Finally, Robert had to make a decision as to which man he needed to pay the money to first. With constant threats from Henley but more trouble if he didn't pay back the lender, Robert decided to hand the boat over to Mr Squires to clear his debt with him.

The country at this time was spiralling into economic crisis. Tourists were staying at home so, with no more bookings at the Warbury guest house, Robert out of work and no money coming in, the Hichens' relationship was put under an enormous strain. Robert had started to drink heavily and when their house was finally taken from them Florence left him, taking the children back to Southampton. She found a house in Shirley Road and, although Robert had followed her to the city, he was not welcome in the family home. For the next two years he tramped around the country, visiting different ports and trying to find work, but as the grip of the Depression tightened and thousands of men were left unemployed, there was little to be had.

All anyone can surmise at this time is that Robert was suffering from an untreated mental illness; he had no job, no money and no house; his family was gone and he was drinking heavily. The alcohol doubtless provided the only thing he had left to block out the pain and memory, the guilt, blame and self-pity. Not only was he suffering with self-loathing, but Robert blamed what had happened to him on another, and that was Harry Henley. Harry had been a rogue and a scoundrel, if he had waited for just a short while longer maybe Robert would have been able to pay him back, but Harry kept threatening Robert and making his life hell. In Robert's mind, Harry had separated him from the one thing he held dear – his family – and the only way he could end this torment and loathing for himself and for Harry was to destroy both. So he set to work. Rooting in the pawn shops and asking on the street and in the many pubs he went to he was finally able to buy a small silver revolver and enough rounds to do the job. Now he would return to Torquay. He had his suicide notes in his pocket and his mind was clearly set.

Early in the evening of 12 November 1933, Robert met his friend Thomas Robert John Holden ('Jack'), a fisherman he had known for thirty years, and they went to a pub together. Jack hadn't seen Robert for two years and he listened as his old friend told him his troubles about the *Queen Mary* and about how Harry had threatened him and forced him out of business. As the two men cradled their tumblers of whiskey, Robert told Jack, 'I have a packet in my pocket and there will be two less in Torquay tonight'. Jack could see Robert was determined. He told his friend not to be so rash, but there was no shaking his resolve. Spending a while longer with his friend of so many years, Robert shook Jack's hand and bade him farewell. He walked up to the Princess Gardens pub where he met Charles Henry Stroud, a docker he had known for a time before he had left Torquay. Stroud asked Robert what he was doing in Torquay and Robert replied, 'I've come to do that bastard in.' Stroud asked him who he meant and Robert told him a condensed version of the story. Robert took the gun out and showed it to his mate. Stroud told

Robert to put it away. 'Henley's not worth swinging for,' he said. 'I'll take your tip, I won't give the hangman a job,' Robert replied and pulled out the small revolver once more. 'This is harder than a boxing glove,' he said, and downed his drink. By now Robert was slurring his words and his eyes were drooping as the whiskey did its work.[38]

They left the pub and as they were walking up the Strand past the memorial clock, Stroud saw Harry on the other side of the road. Harry looked over and squinted, not sure if the stout man on unsteady legs was who he thought it was. Robert had his head bent down and didn't see his enemy. Stroud tried once more to persuade Robert that he was being foolish but he brushed him away, said goodbye and weaved across the main road to where the taxis were waiting for fares. Robert peered through the windows of each one and finally recognised Leslie Scrivings, another friend from the past. Robert asked him to drive to No.6 Happaway Court, Stentiford Hill, the home of Harry Henley. By the time they had got to Stentiford Hill, however, it was obvious that Scrivings' taxi wouldn't make it up the sharp incline, so he parked up outside the Alpine Inn and the two men got out. The hill was steep and Scrivings had to help Robert by holding on to his arm for most of the way. He didn't know the reason for Robert's visit to Happaway Court.

They entered the courtyard and in the corner was No.6. Stroud walked with Robert to the door. 'Well Bob,' Scrivings said, 'I'll see you between 11 and 12 OK?' Then he left. It was now 10.30p.m. Robert stood at the door. He knocked twice, hard. The door finally opened and the men faced each other. In the time it had taken intoxicated Robert to get there, Harry Henley had beaten him home. 'Do you know me Harry?' Robert did his best to stand tall and looked unblinking into the eyes of his tormentor. 'Yes Robert, I know you, what are you doing here at this time of night?' Harry replied. 'I am on the floor and I want you to pick me up,' Robert said. 'How do you expect me to pick you up when you owe me money?' Henry asked standing there, sober and warm in his house with not a care in the world. 'It's through the drink I am like this,' Robert slurred. 'I wouldn't give you a halfpenny if you were lying in the gutter,' Harry sneered. 'If you were sober, I'd give you the thrashing you deserve.'

Robert then reached into his pocket. Harry saw the glint of something small and silver in his hand. Robert lifted his arm and, doing his best to focus, said, 'Take that!' There was a flash and Robert thought he had found his target, but the bullet had glanced off the side of Harry's head above his ear. Harry reached up with his right arm as Robert fired again, but Harry was easily able to anticipate the shot and he threw a punch at Robert, hitting him squarely on the jaw. He staggered back a few steps with Harry coming at him, a good foot in height taller, with his arm swung back, blood spilling from his head wound. Robert's head snapped back as Harry's big fist drove into his chin once more and he collapsed on the ground. Harry looked back at the crumpled figure on the cobbled yard and then staggered out and down the hill towards the police station.

Robert came round, the whiskey no doubt masking the pain in his head and jaw. He slowly pulled himself to his feet and with his gun in his hand he lurched out into the night after Harry. He made it 30yds down the hill then collapsed again onto the pathway. Taking the silver revolver he put it to his temple, squeezed the trigger and click … click, click. The gun was empty. He must have felt a complete failure. He hadn't killed Harry and he was still alive too. Lying back in the gutter, Robert looked up until the world started to fade as he lost consciousness.

Back at Happaway Court Thomas Dart had heard the commotion, argument and then the two gunshots. As he parted his curtains from his bedroom window he saw Robert get to his feet and stagger out of the yard. Quickly dressing, Thomas pulled on his boots and strode out to Stentiford Hill. He saw Robert put the gun to his head and try to blow his brains out and then collapse. Running to the prone figure he took the gun out of Robert's hand and pocketed it. Another man, Richard Medway, had been returning home when he saw Harry coming down the hill, blood soaking the side of his head, hurrying on towards the nearby police station. He reached the scene where Robert was mumbling and cursing, 'The bastard took my launch, is he dead?'

It wasn't long before two policemen arrived. The gun was handed to one of the officers and then they half walked, half dragged Robert down the hill to the station. Harry was in another room being seen by the police doctor. The wound, although still bleeding, was not serious and bandages were wound round his head.

Robert was cautioned and then charged with attempted murder and put in a cell. Superintendent Martin sat on a chair in front of him and warned him not to say anything until he had counsel, but Robert was babbling and moaning: 'I have had it on my mind for a long time … The villain has robbed me … He is a dirty rat and I hope he is dead … He threatened me once and I walked away … I would do it again if I had the chance.' Robert was put in a cell for the night to sleep off the effects of the whiskey. In the early hours he must have found something sharp in his cell and tried to cut his wrists and then, failing that, had slipped into a booze-fuelled stupor.

Robert had been kept on remand at Devon County Jail for more than two weeks, then on 29 November he was taken to the Court at Winchester Assizes for his trial. Florence had been informed by letter and was waiting outside the court rooms with the boys Bob and Freddie. Mr Justice du Parq was the Lord Chief Justice, with Mr Malcom acting on Robert's defence and Mr Laskey for the prosecution. Robert sat so low in his seat that only the top of his head was showing. His wrists had been bandaged and his head was bowed far down on to his chest. Harry Henley stood in the witness box, head also swathed in bandages, but alert and taking a keen interest in proceedings. Before the witnesses were called, two letters were produced in evidence and they were read out in court. The first had been written by Robert in Newton Abbot to the editor of the *Sunday Chronicle*:

> There will be more to add to my book story – Mr Blackey has got it – the last man at the wheel of the ill-fated liner Titanic, the world's greatest sea disaster. I am quite sane but tonight I shall shoot myself, this time I have got my man at Torquay. He stole my launch. I paid £100 for it. I have no living, my home is gone and my wife and children are in Southampton somewhere, the best wife in the world, bless her. If you have anything to give for my story, find her out, Florence Hichens, two sons, one with a leg off, 20, the other aged 9. I have been determined to do this robber in but until now, I could not get a gun. So goodbye to you …

The second letter produced was to his younger brother William:

> My dear little brother. Just a last note to you. You may come and identify my body as your brother. My home is gone. No dole,

no pension, can't get an officer's berth. Result: death by my own hand. Dear brother, convey my kind feelings to all the family. I am no coward but this robber has to go as well. He stole my launch and my living. You can read this letter last. All love to you all. Your loving brother, Robert.

After hearing the letters read out Robert leapt to his feet shouting: 'I would do it ten times over if I could. I would brain the mongrel!' He was persuaded to sit down by a police officer. When Harry was giving his evidence Robert broke down in tears and started to mumble. 'I can't stand it my dear fellows. It is too much for me; I feel my brain will burst.' Then he started to repeat over and over, 'I spell my name with three letters, M.A.N.'

Jack, Medway, Stroud, Dart and Scrivings all gave their evidence. Harry had missed out the bit where he had threatened to thrash Robert, but Medway had heard this and told the court. Still, the case was clear. With the witnesses questioned and the evidence given, it was time for the barrister for the defence to make his statement to the jury. In addressing the jury, Mr Wright said that these were very grave charges but that there were peculiar features. He asked the jury to see that the prisoner's state of mind at the time of the act was such he could not realise what he was doing, and although he committed the act, his mind did not go with it. The jury were entitled to ask themselves if the prisoner was so dethroned by drink that he was incapable of informing intent to murder. They must consider the type of man with whom they were dealing, he said; a man who was at the helm of the famous ship *Titanic* in 1912. When they thought of a man who had gone through that terrible ordeal and they realised he had been sinking lower and lower through drink, brought on by being so down and out, Mr Wright beseeched them, were they not dealing with a man who was not a healthy, normal individual?

He submitted that they were dealing with a man of abnormal mind. He did not say that Robert was insane, but that they should look with the greatest care and with the greatest understanding at the condition of his mind. He invited the jury to come to the conclusion that the prisoner was not in a fit state to form the terrible intention to murder. By doing that, he believed they would be doing the greatest act of fair play and justice that had been done to him for many years and he would go forth from the court with a new life and new hope. His Lordship in his address said there could be no doubt in the mind of anybody who had listened to the case that the prisoner had pointed a loaded gun at Henley and pulled the trigger, and that had the bullet gone only a quarter of an inch to the right, Henley would now have been a dead man. If they were dealing with a sane man there was the simple rule in law that a man must be presumed to intend the natural consequence of the act that he did. He reiterated that it was not suggested in this case that the defendant was not sane. In his review of the evidence, His Lordship pointed out that the letters showed that the defendant had made up his mind to take the action that he did.

The jury found Robert guilty of attempted murder. Police Sergeant Hutchings, on Robert's behalf, said that the defendant had been a merchant seaman and had served with the Royal Naval Reserves in the First World War and his service character was very good. Mr Wright then asked His Lordship to have regard for the fact that they had before them a broken man. He asked him to exercise his discretion and blend mercy with justice as far as he thought right and to inflict such sentence as would not crush him because he was very much down. His Lordship, in turn, told the prisoner that he knew as well as anyone in court that he was very fortunate not to be tried for murder. He went on to say that it was difficult to know to what extent he ought to allow himself to be influenced by some matters, so well-put by counsel for the defence, because this was a terrible offence. He had no doubt that drink was the cause of all his troubles. And he knew that although Robert was perfectly sane and in law was able to form an intention, his mind was *not* perhaps in the fullest degree normal, and because he paid attention to his good character he was going to pass a lighter sentence than was usual. The least sentence he could pass was that he be kept in penal servitude for five years. At this point Robert asked if he would be able to see his wife and children and this was granted.

Robert served his five years at Parkhurst Prison on the Isle of Wight. Florence visited him and his daughter, Ivy Doreen, sent her betrothed to ask her father for permission to marry, which he agreed. In the summer of 1937 Robert was released.

14

THE *ENGLISH TRADER*

During his internment Robert and Florence must have patched up their relationship as when he was freed they lived together again, at Shirley Road with only Freddie still at home at fourteen. Bob had his own place having left home some time before. They had two years together before Florence, having complained of severe headaches, received the terrible news that she had a brain tumour. They spoke about surgery to remove the cancer but the risks were very high and Robert was so desperate to spend the remaining time with his wife, having been parted from her for so long, that he couldn't agree to surgery. With help from friends, Robert and Freddie nursed Florence as best they could until she needed extra care and was moved to a nursing home in St Mary's, where she eventually died on 23 March 1940. Freddie moved in with Bob for a while and then went to live with his Aunty Phyllis. Robert couldn't bear to stay at the house either, and the ageing sailor decided to return to the sea for what would be his last voyage.[39]

The *English Trader* was a 3,753-ton cargo ship with two single-ended boilers and a triple expansion reciprocating steam engine, owned by the Trader Navigation Company. She was special in that she had a revolutionary hull design called ARCFORM which increased her stability and improved her fuel consumption. This was designed by Joseph Isherwood, who would later receive a knighthood for his contribution to the maritime industry. Three years before Robert joined her she had run aground off the Devon coast and the only way to free her had been to cut her in half and tow her remaining aft part into Dartmouth harbour. A new bow section was grafted on to her, but this engineering procedure affected her stability and what had been thought of as a safe and comfortable ship to sail on now developed into a vessel that was unable to maintain an even keel for any length of time. A slight swell was enough to get her pitching badly, and in rough weather a 30° roll was not uncommon, so for the crew of the 'temperamental lady', a strong stomach was a must.

These were dangerous times for the crews of the Merchant Navy. Britain needed to see 125 freighters into her ports every week, bringing vital supplies from across the north and south Atlantic. The Second World War was in its second year; the sky was filled with German fighters and bombers and the seas infested with U-boat wolf packs who discharged a variety of mines in a bid to destroy the ships and so cripple trade. Many vessels sailed in convoys, protected by destroyers and scouts, but 72 per cent of them still had to sail alone and their protection would be the brave gunners on deck who kept a vigilant watch on the skies above and the sea below. Of the forty-three crew on the *English Trader*, eleven were gunners; one of which was a man Robert became friends with called William Hickson. Upon joining the ship William couldn't believe his good fortune when he discovered she was armed with a 4in breech-loading semi-automatic gun: only two others existed in the whole of the Merchant Navy at that time. There was also a 12lb anti-aircraft gun and a Lewis machine-gun. It was William's job to supervise the gun deck, the watches and discipline of the other gunners, service the equipment and teach four other seamen how to man the guns if necessary.

Robert had joined the *English Trader* as third mate on 23 May 1940 in Liverpool. They sailed up the east coast keeping watch for the enemy U-boats that patrolled there, then up to Scotland and down to Hull where they picked up their cargo of 7,000 tons of coal for the long voyage to Freetown, Sierra Leone, via Montevideo, Buenos Aries. Not one week into the voyage, while steaming at their normal speed of 8 knots, a thirty-year-old seaman called James Bolger was down in lower hold No.3 when there was some sort of commotion. Shouts were heard: 'Watch out below!' Then there was a crash of the hatch falling down, which somehow hit Bolger on the head, killing him instantly. He was taken off the ship at Greenock. Their journey continued down the east coast towards Southend in Essex, escorting some unarmed French fishing trawlers, but they soon found themselves in trouble as they ran into a British minefield and had to anchor and wait for a patrol to guide them out. Leaving the trawlers, they headed for the River Plate in Buenos Aries.

It was a horrible trip across the north Atlantic for everyone on board, with hardly any sleep for the whole crew. The ship was rolling and pitching, continually battling with heavy seas. Robert was constantly soaked to the skin even in his weather gear, and with only short breaks in between shifts as huge waves crashed on the sides of the ship, he was soon exhausted. The threat of enemy attack was never far away either. One day, while William Hickson was on the gun deck, he saw a suspicious pole moving through the water in the distance. He telephoned the bridge, but after getting no response he took it on himself to open fire on the U-boat. The problem was, however, that it wasn't a U-boat but another freighter, far up ahead, trailing a fog buoy made out of a barrel and a spout which helped the convoy when visibility was poor. If it wasn't for the frantic lamp signals, William might have ended up blowing up one of their ships. Meekly going to report what he had done to Captain Harkness, he was very relieved when the skipper praised him for his diligence. There were frequent subsequent sightings of U-boats in the distance, but the *English Trader* managed to avoid any direct contact, although the low buzzing ahead of German Commerce Raiders and Focke Wulf Condors was never far away.

By 10 July they were steaming in the seas of the south Atlantic when smoke was seen coming out from No.4 hatch. In an eerie echo of *Titanic*, a fire had been discovered due to the coal self-combusting in the hold, and the stokers were doing all they could to keep it under control. The noxious fumes from the burning coal made the atmosphere almost unbearable. Robert started to complain of breathing problems and became bronchial and ill. Over the coming days, with the situation getting worse in the bunkers below, Robert's temperature rose to 99°F and he found it impossible to keep food down. On the surface once again, the *English Trader* faced severe gales. In her bowels the firemen did the best they could. With the surface conditions worsening the crew could do nothing more but batten down the hatches and ride out the storm.

They sailed into Montevideo, Buenos Aires, on 24 July and Lloyds surveyors came aboard to assess the situation. The fire had burnt a 3ft hole in one of the wooden bulkheads and thousands of tons of coal, which was rapidly turning into coke, was being dampened by having water played on it from above. Finally the gases given off from the coal set off a chemical reaction, and in the confines of the hold there was suddenly an explosion. No.2 hatch blew from its hinges 30ft into the air and the force of the blast also blew part of a gangplank skywards. It fell back to earth but not before catching Second Officer Frank Lond on the back of his head. He slumped to the floor, blood pouring from a wicked gash, and was immediately rushed to a British hospital. At first they thought the stitches they put in would be enough to aid his recovery, but the doctors discovered he had compression on the brain and he could not return to England on the ship.

Eventually the fire was put out and a shipment of grain was taken on board. The *English Trader* made its way up the River Plate and berthed at Ibicuy. Robert was seriously ill but his temperature had come down and with Lond in hospital he needed to get back to work to support the other officers and his captain. In Santa Fe the doctor was called again as one of the crew had lumbago, another grippe, which was a type of 'flu. He offered to check Robert over but he refused any examination or treatment. It was the end of August by the time they made it to Freetown to deliver the coal and then they were ready to go home. They would be making port in Aberdeen in three weeks' time.

Yet another mighty storm on their homeward journey in the north Atlantic washed off a lifeboat, damaging the davits, and then another wave claimed a port sally boat and a load of equipment. In a short reprieve from the bad weather, Robert was up on deck, sitting on No.4 hatch, enjoying some welcome sunshine with the friend he had made on the voyage, the gunner William Hickson. Taking a nip from his whiskey flask and passing it to William, Robert said almost casually, 'I shall not live to see England again'. William laughed and scotched the idea, but Robert insisted he knew his own mind best. They carried on their easy companionship and then went back to their duties. William, thinking nothing of Robert's musings and looking forward to reaching Scotland in a few days' time, forgot about their conversation. At last the long trip had come to an end and the *English Trader* was moored off the coast of Aberdeen, waiting to unload, when First Mate Leonard Thomas came up to William, very upset, with bad news for the gunner: Robert was dead. Just three days after they had shared a dram together his weather-beaten friend, with his Cornish lilt and incredible tale of being the last man at the wheel of the *Titanic*, had died of heart failure. His premonition had come true.

On 23 September, the day Robert finally joined his beloved Florence, two letters were written by the crew on the *English Trader*. The following was the statement made by Assistant Steward Jack Parker:

> This is to certify that, in my opinion, Mr Hichens was in a very depressed state when he first joined the ship in Liverpool. I heard him say often that he had recently lost his wife and that he wished he was with her. He also said his heart was very bad and that he thought this would be his last trip to sea.
>
> About four or five days ago when we were having bad weather at sea he went on watch at 8am but shortly afterwards he returned to his room and told me that he felt very ill. Since that time I have gone to him every meal-time and asked him what he wanted to eat but he refused everything. The Chief Steward and the Master tried to coax him to have porridge or soup but he would only drink water or coffee. At 9.30am this morning I went to clean his room and found him sitting upright on his settee, eyes closed. I tried to wake him but could not so I covered him in blankets.

A statement written by Chief Steward Arthur Drinkwater begins in a similar way, but adds, 'I went with the Master to see how Mr Hichens was and found him very weak. I fed him with small amounts of brandy on a teaspoon and at 10.20 am he died in the presence of the Master and myself.'

Robert's body was taken by tender to a mortuary in Aberdeen. The paperwork was filled out, the records taken and Robert disappeared once again. His family tried very hard over the years to find out what happened to his body and we are still looking. Maybe one day whoever is left will be able to lay a wreath somewhere out at sea or in a Scottish graveyard and pay their respects to the last man at the wheel of *Titanic*.

EPILOGUE

Phyllis May was Robert's third daughter, known as the *Titanic* baby, and she was my grandmother. She had three sons with her first husband Alf Russell: Graham, Bev and Warner. Bev is my father. I remember going to stay at her house in Telford, Staffordshire, which she shared with her third husband, John Waters, who was Irish and doted on Phyllis and their son James. There were horse brasses around the fireplace and a canary which sang its heart out in its cage in the window. In the back room, I remember a huge glass bowl filled with match books. I started my own collection a few years ago and never got higher than an inch in my glass bowl. I'll never forget how pitch black it was in the tiny box room I slept in, snuggled up in a 'proper' bed with sheets, blankets and a satin eiderdown.

My only other memory of Phyllis was her sitting up in bed in St Thomas's Hospital in London when she was very ill with stomach cancer. I couldn't tell she was so poorly as she looked beautiful, her hair still dark and curly, framing her smiling face which was never without makeup, with her lovely nightdress and perfectly manicured nails. My brother John and I pushed each other up and down the ward in a wheelchair and when we looked out of the large windows we saw the Thames flowing by and giant white kitten footprints on the pavement below, put there for a classic episode of our favourite TV programme *The Goodies*. Sadly, Phyllis died soon after; it was 1976 and I was eleven.

It was Alf Russell who first told me about Robert Hichens. Our family had moved to Surrey and we would travel down to Southampton to meet up with all our relatives three or four times a year. One of our favourite pubs was the Sir John Barleycorn in Cadnam where Phyllis had worked many years ago. Grandad told me that Robert had been at the wheel of the *Titanic* when it had hit the iceberg, and had later shot a man and had gone to prison. Something else that stuck in my mind was that he told me Robert's nickname was 'Banjo Bob'. It was only recently, when I visited Newlyn, that I learnt about the importance of nicknames. I was in the Newlyn Archive Centre where a gentleman explained that he was compiling a book of local nicknames and their origins. Many men from the town were given them for life, even when the original reason for being given them was long forgotten. Robert's brother William (Willie) was known as 'Walloper Down' for his ability to drink his beer very quickly, and a cousin was called Joe 'Pastie' after the famous Cornish meat pie. Whether Robert ever played a banjo doesn't seem important but 'Banjo Bob' was his nickname and many of his friends just called him Bob.

In April 2003 I went to a *Titanic* exhibition in Southampton with my family organised by Phil Gowan, well-known historian and major contributor of articles for Encyclopedia Titanica. I bought a biscuit tin with the *Queen Mary* on it then spent ages staring at a woman who was covered from head to toe in tattoos depicting everything relating to *Titanic*: icebergs, ships sinking, the White Star Line flag, even Captain Smith on a large, bare shoulder. I queued for ages with my mother to meet and get an autograph from Millvina Dean. She was very slim, had a lovely curly wig, big glasses and pink lipstick and was thoroughly enjoying all the fuss. Millvina had been a baby when she was handed over in a sack to her mother in one of the lifeboats, and was the oldest survivor of the disaster until 2010 when she passed away.

Phil Gowan, with the help of Brian Meister, set about to discover more about Robert and in 2001 Phil wrote an excellent article entitled, 'Whatever Happened to Robert Hichens?' An enormous amount of time and effort had been put into the mini biography and it was from this that I made the decision to write my book. Following on from Phil's research has been a big challenge. Robert and Florence were private people and passed little information down to their children, and most of *their* children had little interest or knowledge of their ancestor. My father has a vague memory of jumping on Florence's bed, breaking some china and getting chased out of the house. I felt very privileged to visit Dorothy Hichens, or 'Ching' as she prefers to be called. She is the wife of Robert's youngest son Freddie, and she was able to tell me something about the relationship he had with his father. It was Ching who told me how much Freddie loved his dad and about Robert's trips to China and the beautiful pottery he brought back. Freddie had never really gotten over the death of his father and the complicated feelings he had for him, and in later life he too had suffered with the demon drink which led to the couple separating, although they remained friends.

I also had a great visit with Robert's niece Barbara and her husband Peter Clarke in Torquay. Barbara told me of the time she had met her uncle Robert. He was wearing a navy-blue hat and navy jumper and had patted her on the head saying, 'You're a lovely looking maid' which was typical of the way he spoke. Spending a week with my newly discovered family in Newlyn gave me the opportunity to meet lots of Hichenses. They could not have made me more welcome, and their dry sense of humour and warm, generous nature was reflected in everyone I met in Newlyn, which gave me a real feel of what a tight-knit community it continues to be.

There is a great deal of information at Southampton City Library and one of the largest collections of *Titanic*-related literature I have seen. Often there was disappointment: Southampton was bombed in the Blitz of the Second World War and much of the beautiful architecture has been replaced with concrete high-rise buildings and road-improvement schemes. James Street was demolished in the 1960s and a low-level housing development was built in its place. St Mary's Street, once a bustling and colourful thoroughfare with shops and trams and the Kingsland Square Market, has little to show now; sadly it too looks unloved with boarded-up shop fronts, graffiti, sports bars and pound arcades in its place. Standing at berth No.44 where *Titanic* sailed from is very special, you just need a lot of imagination to cast yourself back to Wednesday 10 April 1912 and imagine the band playing, flags waving and the whistles of the train and the ship blowing over the port as the huge, beautiful liner made ready to steam away on her maiden voyage. Newlyn is still steeped in history although sadly St Peter's Square was flattened and turned into a car park, as was Happaway Court in Torquay where Robert came face to face with his adversary, Harry Henley.

Locating crew lists and the ships Robert served on was also tricky. In 1966 the Registry General of Shipping and Seamen ran out of storage space and countless boxes of archives were lost or shared amongst libraries, maritime museums or returned to the ships' owners. Many records were sent to a large maritime archive unit based in Newfoundland. Were it not for the persistence of research-ers like Inger Shiel who was able to track down some of the vessels he sailed on, I would have come to a dead end on many occasions. One of the most fascinating experiences I had was visiting the National Archives in Kew, Richmond. I was led into a supervised room and laid out before me was the log of Robert's last voyage, written by his captain, Jack Harkness. The details of the storms and the coal fires and the poignant last days of Robert's life were very emotional for me to read. They confirmed what I had read in a wonderful little book from an obscure bookseller called *The Loss of The English Trader* by Cyril Jolly where the gunner, William Hickson, had sat with Robert and spoken about his prophecy and the adventures they'd had on their way to the River Plate.

I hope in writing this book I have been able to put the record straight about Robert Hichens and to give some explanation as to what it was like to be a lower-ranking crewman in 1912 with the hierarchy, class system and many trials a man like him had to face. Throughout his life Robert had worked hard and had done his best to provide for his family. With no support system after the *Titanic* disaster he had to face the horrors he had witnessed, the scorn of his peers, the jibes from the people he had saved and the rejection of his employers – alone. It is no real surprise that his life turned out the way it did. I thought long and hard before taking the decision to use Thomas Garvey's letter and its account of Robert's confession as the basis for his experience on *Titanic*. There was an honesty in what Thomas wrote that I didn't see in the testimonies given by the witnesses at the inquiries. And finally: was Robert a coward and a bully? Maybe I'm biased, but I don't think he was. I am proud of what he *did* achieve and sympathetic to what he went through; putting his life in print for others to see is the most fulfilling and worthwhile cause I have had the privilege to undertake.

APPENDIX

WHAT HAPPENED TO ...?

Charles Herbert Lightoller

Lightoller was never made captain of a ship with the White Star Line even though he defended the shipping company during the inquiries; he did, however, command two ships during wartime service in the First World War. During the Second World War he took part in the Dunkirk evacuation, rescuing over 100 troops from the beaches in France using his yacht *Sandowner*. In later life he raised chickens, opened a boarding house for a while and finally owned a boatyard in Twickenham, Surrey. He died in 1952 at the age of seventy-eight of heart and lung disease.

Margaret Tobin Brown

Margaret Tobin 'Molly' Brown, for a brief moment, reached the echelons of high society in her home town of Denver, Colorado, as a result of the press exposure generated by her *Titanic* experience. She was even invited to lunch with the Sacred Thirty-Six, a group of first-generation aristocracy she had tried to be a member of for years, but her inclusion would be short-lived. Her pretentiousness and eccentricity kept her from being truly accepted. She was separated from her husband and when he died he left no will, leading to acrimonious court battles over money between Molly and her son and daughter. Over the years Molly did much for charitable causes and played an important role in reforming juvenile delinquents. Her flamboyancy and uniqueness led her character to be epitomised in Broadway musicals and the 1950 film *The Unsinkable Molly Brown* with Debbie Reynolds, and she will be best remembered recently for her portrayal in James Cameron's film *Titanic*. Wherever Molly Brown's character appeared, Robert Hichens would be there too. Margaret Tobin Brown died on 25 October 1932, aged sixty-five, in a hotel in New York of a brain haemorrhage following the discovery of a tumour.

Frederick Fleet

Fleet was believed to have been rewarded by the White Star Line for his secrecy about the early ice warnings with a pension for life. He served briefly on *Titanic*'s sister ship *Olympic*, but his link to *Titanic* was seen as an embarrassment and he left, continuing his life on the sea with other shipping lines. In 1936 he returned to dry land and worked for Harland and Wolff shipbuilders and later sold newspapers on the streets of Southampton. He carried the guilt of his *Titanic* experience for life. When his wife died he felt he had nothing left to live for and was found hanged in his garden on a clothesline on 10 January 1965. He was buried in a pauper's grave until, with donations from Titanic Historical Society, a headstone was put in its place.

Major Arthur Peuchen

Peuchen went to great lengths to discredit Captain Smith after the disaster and made various complaints about what he thought were a poorly trained crew. In Toronto, Canada, he was maligned as a coward, partly because he was thought of as too self-satisfied. After commanding a battalion in the First World War, he returned to his hometown then, in his later life, bad investments led him to losing the majority of his wealth. He died at his home on 7 December 1926, aged seventy.

Bruce Ismay

Ismay was criticised by surviving passengers and hounded by the press for leaving the stricken *Titanic*. He was branded a coward by many, although some surviving crew maintained that he followed the 'women and children first' rule. He returned to England on the *Adriatic* with the officers and having given evidence once again at the British Inquiry he kept a low profile and in 1913 resigned as chairman of White Star Line and president of International Mercantile Marine. In later life he developed diabetes which resulted in partial amputation of his right leg and he died in Liverpool of a cerebal thrombosis at the age of seventy-four.

The *English Trader*

The *English Trader* was to take her last voyage in October 1941. Loaded with a mixed cargo bound for Kenya, the ship sailed from London and up the east coast as the English Channel was far too dangerous to cross. The ship was part of a convoy of twenty freighters called EC90. Not long into the voyage the *English Trader* was lagging far behind, steaming at a pathetic 4 knots with a serious engine problem, and as night approached the convoy in front came under fierce fire from enemy aircraft. Before long a German Dornier bomber spotted them and came in for the attack. Gunner William Hickson jumped into position at the Lewis gun and fired off a round of ammunition, scoring a hit on the bomber's fuselage. It swooped away but not before discharging two bombs which exploded a few yards from their ship in huge plumes of white foam. HMS *Vesper*, a destroyer sent with the convoy as protection, came to the rescue and saw off the Dornier as it came for a second try.

The *English Trader* continued up the coast and was passing Yarmouth when, on reaching Hammond Knoll, she got caught in a strong ebbing tide and became stuck fast on the sand bank with no hope of freeing herself. The convoy had to continue without her, leaving the stricken steamer a sitting duck. But it wasn't further attack that would be their downfall. In a few hours the seas grew rough around them until huge waves began to batter the freighter. What followed became a famous, desperate attempt by the crew of a Cromer lifeboat commanded by Coxswain Henry Blogg to save the men trapped on the grounded vessel. Three men were washed overboard to their deaths and a further five men from the lifeboat fell into the sea but were rescued (although one succumbed to exposure shortly after). It took five attempts and thirty-six hours in enormous seas before finally the winds died and the remaining men were taken off the 'temperamental lady', including gunner William Hickson. As they left for shore they took one last look at the *English Trader* as she made her final curtain call before disappearing beneath the waves.

Newlyn

Newlyn has changed a great deal since Robert was there and much of the population now are not indigenous. In 1937 the larger council of Penzance pushed for areas in Newlyn to be demolished under a slum-clearance scheme. Many families who had lived there for generations, as well as the artists, were up in arms and a plan to save the town was put in place. In an epic journey to stop the proposal a fishing boat called the *Rosebud* left with a petition and sailed to London and up the Thames, the fishermen arriving at the Houses of Parliament to much media interest. The result of handing over the petition to Government was successful at the time and a conservation order was agreed. This did not, however, prevent the area of St Peter's Square where Robert's family lived being flattened and they, with all the other families, were relocated far up the hill to the newly built Gwavas Estate (where some Hichens' descendants still reside). Much can still be enjoyed in the town: watching the fishing boats come in to land their catch; wandering the pretty cobbled lanes the artists so loved; attending Sunday service at the Methodist church; or just standing on the cliff looking out to sea at St Michael's Mount where Robert and his kin once stood, more than 100 years ago.

The Hichens Family

Edna Hichens married Bernard McKno and they successfully ran two pub/restaurants in Southampton with their daughters Vivian and Brenda. Edna died of breast cancer at the age of forty-nine in 1957. Frances and her partner, Percy Kelsey, lived in Middlesex and Southampton and had three children: Barry, Noel and Gloria. I was lucky enough to meet Gloria and her daughter Sara when they came for lunch, and Gloria kindly gave me a copy of the telegram letting the family know about Florence's death. Frances also died of cancer in 1992, aged eighty-two. Ivy Doreen (Babe) married Fred Woolgar and they had two children: Paul and Sue. Babe died of breast cancer in 1973, aged fifty-eight. Robert (Bob) had been in a tram accident when he was a boy and had his leg amputated. He never married but had a number of girlfriends. He was an accomplished pianist and would travel the bars with Freddie – who was devilishly handsome and had a voice like Bing Crosby. Bob died of heart failure in 1971, aged fifty. Freddie had always been an entrepreneur and had many businesses, flooring being his most successful. Ching, his ex-wife, described him as a loveable rogue with a winning smile. They were to have three children: Janette, Robert and Frederick. In later life, when Freddie and Ching had separated, Freddie went to live with one of his sons for a while and then he too died, in 1985, aged sixty, of heart and lung disease.

Titanic

Titanic rests 2 miles deep on the bottom of the north Atlantic in two pieces. The 1997 film *Titanic* depicts dramatic scenes of the ship tearing apart, with the stern falling back to sea before finally rising up and then slowly making her final descent. On the night of the disaster some witnesses believed *Titanic* sunk in one piece, others that she broke in two. It was not until 1985 that a marine exploration team, headed by Robert Ballard, showed that *Titanic* did in fact break in half in her final minutes. One hundred years after her sinking, reports also tell of microscopic bugs feasting on her rusty iron hull. On her upcoming centenary anniversary, a fleet of cruise ships and other vessels will cluster over the exact sport the luxury liner foundered. The fleet's passengers will be ancestors of those who perished and the many hundreds of followers who continue to be in awe of the mighty leviathan.

ENDNOTES

Introduction

1   That particular rebuke was in fact delivered by a steward in lifeboat 8. First-class passenger Colonel Archibald Gracie interviewed many survivors after the disaster and this, plus many other explicit accounts, would be used for his highly acclaimed 1913 book *Titanic, A Survivor's Story*.

2   Professor Kenneth Plummer from Exeter University advised me on the complicated subjects of memory and life writing.

2   Southampton

3   As described in the book *Chapel and Northam: An Oral History of Southampton Dockland Communities* compiled by Sheila Jemima.

3   Setting Sail

4   As reported on the maiden voyage of the *Adriatic* in New York in 1907. Source: 'Officers of the *Titanic*' by Chris Diano 1998 and webTitanic.com.

5   As described in his biography, *Titanic Voyager*.

4   The First Four Days

6   From an article by Art Braunschweiger and Scott Andrews, Titanic Research and Modelling Association.

7   Researched from *Titanic R.I.P.* by Diane Bristow.

5   'Ice, right ahead!'

8   For this conversation and the subsequent sequence of events leading up to and following the collision I used research from the US *Titanic* Inquiry and the Thomas Garvey letter.

9   *New York Times*, Tuesday 23 April. Klein's testimony in Cleveland, Ohio.

10 As stated by their testimonies at the US Inquiry.

11 Early iceberg warnings came from witness statements given after the sinking.

12 Three ice warnings were allegedly reported by Fleet in the lifeboat and aboard *Carpathia*.

13 Fleet reported ringing the bridge and getting no answer. Robert must have heard the phone ring from his position at the wheel.

14 From Robert's confession to Henry Blum in the Thomas Garvey letter. Quite a different account to the sanitised party line he told at the Inquiries.

15 From Luis Klein's report in *New York Times*, 23 April and his testimony in Cleveland.

16 Claimed to have been heard by witnesses but there is no mention of the 'Hard-a-port' order in Robert's testimonies.

17 Leslie Reade's interview with Frederick Fleet in his book *The Ship that Stood Still*.

18 FromFleet's testimony at the British Inquiry.

19 Boxhall testifies to hearing 'Hard-a-port' order at US/British Inquiries.

20 As above.

21 For the sequence of events leading up to and following the collision I used research from the US Titanic Inquiry.

6 Lifeboat 6

22 Information on Margaret Tobin Brown and other passengers' actions has been researched from affidavits or biographies of the people involved and from testimonies of witnesses at the Inquiries.

23 Information taken from affidavits and biographies of the people involved.

24 Lightoller maintained throughout his testimonies that the atmosphere remained quiet and calm.

7 Rescue

25 City Heritage Collection from the book *Titanic Voices*.

26 As told by Molly Brown to Archibald Gracie for his book *Titanic, A Survivor's Story* and in Kristen Iverson's book *Molly Brown, Unravelling the Myth*.

27 Research from author and historian George Behe.

28 From an account written by Howard Chapin.

8 New York

29 This account of *Titanic*'s arrival in New York was primarily researched from Wynn Craig Wade's book *The Titanic, End of a Dream*.

30 Account as described by Wynn Craig Wade in his book *The Titanic, End of a Dream*.

31 This information was researched from Diane Bristow's book *Titanic, R.I.P.* in which Fleet was said to have told acquaintances about the bribe years later.

32 His wife had left him one year after their marriage perhaps following a scandal regarding his drinking habits. Researched from David Lee's family notes on Encyclopedia Titanica message board.

9 New York Hearings

33 Researched from a biography written by Michele Arsenault and Paula Martens.

34 Lightoller admitted to applying the 'whitewash brush' on different occassions for biographies written about him. To whitewash means to cover up unpleasant facts.

10 Move to Washington

35 There is much debate about which officer was seen shooting himself. Best described in Bill Wormstedt's work 'Shots in the Dark' on wormstedt.com.

36 The story of Luis Klein seeing officers drunk, the fact that he doesn't appear on the particulars of engagement and that he disappeared without trace in New York has provided much debate amongst researchers, some of whom believe he wasn't even on *Titanic*.

11 Homecoming

37 Researched from Senan Maloney's article 'Holy Grail – Missing Dispositions', on Encyclopedia Titanica.com

13 Harry Henley

38 This account of what happened between Robert and Harry Henley was researched from correspondents who were in court and followed the case reporting for the *Torquay Times* newspaper and the *South Devon Journal*.

14 The *English Trader*

39 From a gem of a book called *The Loss of the English Trader* by Cyril Jolly, and from the captain's log researched at The National Archives, I was able to retell the story of Robert's final adventure.

BIBLIOGRAPHY

Books

Bancroft, Caroline, *The Unsinkable Molly Brown* (Johnson Publishing Company, US, 1985)

Behe, George, *Titanic, Safety, Speed and Sacrifice* (Transportation Trails, US, 1997)

Bristow, Diane, *Titanic, R.I.P., Can Dead Men Tell Tales* (Harlow Press, NY, UK, 1989)

Brown, Jim, *The Illustrated History of Southampton Suburbs* (The Breedon Books Publishing Co. Ltd, UK, 2004)

Bryceson, Dave, *The Titanic Disaster, As Reported by the British National Press* (W.W. Norton, US, 1997)

Corin, John, *Fisherman's Conflict, The Story of the Newlyn Riots* (Tops'l Books, UK, 1998)

Eaton, John and Haas, Charles, *Titanic, Triumph and Tragedy* (Patrick Stephens, Somerset, UK, 1994)

Gracie, Colonel Archibald, *Titanic, A Survivor's Story* (Alan Sutton Publishing, UK, 1985)

Haisman, David, *Titanic, The Edith Brown Story* (Author House UK Ltd, 2009)

Hyslop, Donald; Forsythe, Alistair and Jemima, Sheila, *Titanic Voices*, (Sutton Publishing, Gloucester, 1997)

Iverson, Kirstin, *Molly Brown, Unravelling The Myth* (Johnson Books, Colorado, 1999)

Jolly, Cyril, *The Loss of The English Trader* (Acorn Editions, UK, 1981)

Kuntz, Tom, *The Titanic Disaster Hearings* (Pocket Books, UK, 1998)

Lomax, Pamela and Hogg, Ron, *Newlyn Before The Artists Came* (Shears and Hogg, UK, 2010)

Lord, Walter, *A Night To Remember* (Owl Books, Henry Holt and Company, NY, 1983)

Lord, Walter, *The Night Lives On* (Penguin Books, NY, UK, 1998)

Lynch, Don and Marshall, Ken, *Titanic, An Illustrated History* (Hodder and Stoughton, UK, 1992)

Maltin, Tim and Aston, Eloise, *101 things you thought you knew about the Titanic, but didn't* (Beautiful Books, UK, 2010)

Nicholson, Juliet, *The Perfect Summer* (John Murray Publishing, UK, 2006)

Reade, Leslie, *The Ship That Stood Still* (Patrick Stephens, Somerset, UK)

Scarth, Alan, *Titanic and Liverpool* (Liverpool University Press, UK, 2009)

Stenson, Patrick, *Titanic Voyager, The Odyssey of C.H. Lightoller* (Halsgrove and Endurance Publishing, UK, 2006)

Wade, Wynn Craig, *The Titanic, End of a Dream* (Penguin Books, NY, 1998)

Woodman, Richard, *More Days, More Dollars, The Universal Bucket Chain 1885–1920* (The History Press, Stroud, UK, 2010)

Articles

Aikman, Chris, 'Titanic Tales' (article on the Douglas family)

Arsenault, Michele and Martens, Paula, *Titanic Lore* (article on Charles Lightoller)

'Elsie Edith Bowerman 1889–1973', and her mother 'Edith Bowerman Chibnall 1864–1953', *Hastings Press*

English Trader Log Book, BT381/1093, 23 May 1940, National Archives

'Feeding the fires, boilers, firemen and trimmers', Titanic Research and Modelling Association

Gowan, Phil and Meister, Brian, 'Whatever Happened to Robert Hichens?', Encyclopedia Titanica

Gowan, Phil, 'Titanic–Titanic' (article on Mr Robert Hichens)

'Helen Churchill Candee' Biography, Encyclopedia Titanica

'HMS Revenge', Wikipedia

'Luis Klein Story', *New York Times*, Tuesday 23 April 1912

Malony, Senan, 'The Missing Dispositions', Encyclopedia Titanica

'Sealing the Lips of Titanic Crew', *New York Times*, Sunday 21 April 1912

'Sensational Attempted Murder Case', *Torquay Times*, 7 November 1933

Shiel, Inger, 'Titanic Quartermaster Robert Hichens and The Royal Naval Reserve', *Atlantic Daily Bulletin* (No.3, 2003)

'Titanic Deck Crew', Encyclopedia Titanica

'Titanic's Seamen at Prayer Service', *New York Times*, Friday 19 April 1912

'Titanic Survivor found guilty of attempted murder', *Torquay Directory, South Devon Journal*, 22 November, 6 December 1933

'To Hold Ismay to the End', *New York Times*, Monday 22 April 1912

'Two of Titanic's men ask for help and get it', *New York Times*, Wednesday 24 April 1912

'Virtual Venice – Amusements' (article on Luis Klein)

'Women Revealed as Heroines', *New York Times*, Saturday 20 April 1912

Wormstedt, Bill and Ottmers, Rob, 'US and British Hearings and ice report', *Titanic Inquiry Project*

Wormstedt, Bill, 'Shots in the Dark' (article on Murdoch's suicide)

THE TITANIC COLLECTIO

THE 100TH ANNIVERSARY OF THE SINKING OF TITANIC 15TH APRIL 201

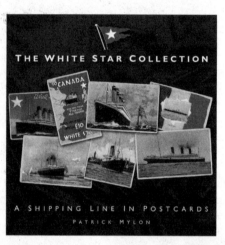

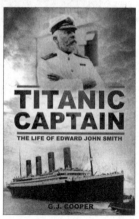

For the full Titanic experience visit The History Press website
and follow the Titanic link **www.thehistorypress.co.uk**
For stories and articles about Titanic, join us on Facebook